UNDERSTANDING CUSTOMER EXPERIENCE MANAGEMENT

DRIVING CUSTOMER SUCCESS

DR. AMRINDER KAUR | MS. RINKU BHARDWAJ

Dedicated to our Family, Associates, and Colleagues for always being there

Contents

Prologue

Meant for Decision Makers, Entrepreneurs, Customer Success Managers, Customer Experience Teams and to all whom "Customer" is important

Foreword

Writing the foreword for this book indeed is an enchanting experience for me. It is not just because of my long association with Rinku and Amrinder but because it is about a topic that is so important in today's landscape. Over the last two years, a robust paradigm has witnessed digital transformation in overall business operations. And this is true for large organizations, MSMEs, and startups alike. However, the most significant afterthought for me, after an unrestrained 2020, 2021, is how Customers and individuals set the experiences in line with expectations.

It catalyzed the paradigm shift as businesses continued to stretch and challenge themselves, and we witnessed the total transformation in overall business operations. Or maybe, in other words, digital transformation was the necessity to survive the blows of the pandemic and complete disruption affecting countries, businesses, and people alike. Heading into 2022, I witness enterprises progressively embracing digital transformation to add a competitive edge to their business strategies. It is also helping with robust positioning in the antagonistic market. I believe Customer Experience with digital transformation was always on the agenda as organizations grew their size and scale and added more innovative features and capabilities to their arsenal. However, the pandemic accelerated the need and pace for businesses. Simultaneously, from the consumers' aspect, I witness that they are gradually embracing technology. It brings ease and convenience to them. Even the government is bringing in more flexible regulations to enable greater technological adoption. It has paved the way for more extraordinary curated experiences for customers with technology as the enabler.

My two decades' experience working with various organizations has made a few revelations valid across organizations of different sizes and markets. First, customer experiences and mapping deliverables around expectations remain critical determinants of brand building to target customer loyalty for business growth with consistent preferences for self-service, personalization, and real-time resolutions. Second, this business growth, brand building, and digital transformation mean the people responsible for managing CX for their organizations must re-consider the consumer landscape and prioritize in new ways viz-a-viz changes in customer base and behavior over the past few years. It won't be wrong if I say that Digital Customer Experience trends will likely gather steam as technology promises to address the challenges and opportunities for enterprises for sustainable growth. And taking customer needs and expectations will be the key to this development. Customers share information about their choices and viewpoints; they have expectations and problems, which becomes a necessary point of view even while designing the products and services. Creating customer-centric strategies is imperative for enterprises, and the inability to act on the feedback puts them on the back front. Lot many times, even when I have been working with different companies, this feedback aspect supported us with ideas for growth, engagement, and innovation.

The customer truly is king, so adopting the right approach to manage customer experiences has significant payoffs – for your customers and your bottom line. Customer Experience can give the brand the differentiation, innovation, and optimum usage of resources for profitability to create a viable and sustainable business amongst their competitor—the way of delivery matters over what is delivered. The way enterprises engage with their customers directly affects sales figures, brand retention value, and differentiation from other brands as it caters to customer requirements by understanding customer behaviors. And this book precisely answers that for you. Every stage in a company, from idea generation to scaling it with processes, service, employee engagement, and governance plans, needs a systematic way to handle it.

This handbook for the decision-makers certainly shall help introspect their customer experience journey. As customers, we also know that our expectations are rising with the available knowledge and choices; hence, organizations have to fasten and align goals and objectives. And I must admit, as decision-makers, we often want a perspective on which initiatives to pick. For example, we think customer relationship management can be done by customer service, or we can manage growth without a strategic governance plan, measuring experience doesn't make a difference, or precisely we know our customer's journey.

The book breaks the myth of the differences and why focusing on the right strategy for a problem can make a difference. I was enthralled that each chapter focused on one concept with plenty of examples to support it. So I can learn about governance by starting right from that chapter per my need. Each chapter is a new start to reflect on. I just wish the readers a good reading time, and I truly hope this book supports the endeavor for the focused customer organization. It means more growth, innovation, brand building, and products/services that truly matter. You can build a 360-degree view of customers with the integrated data flow by understanding your customers and creating a customer journey map to develop an emotional connection of customers with your brand. And I should specifically talk about the impact of measurement, which is pivotal to tracking various metrics/KPIs to see the gap and growth with our initiatives to reach our goals. Metrics give numbers to specific vague interactions, behaviors, and deliverables and are more prominent as a multitude of data is created across multiple channels and customer journey touchpoints. The measures, frameworks, and concepts on CX can make a difference as you work to build a customer-centric organization. I warmly congratulate the authors and welcome readers on reading, reflecting, and learning from the handbook to implement and create organizations that matter. Rachana Chowdhary (Ms. Rachana Chowdhary is the Global Media & Marketing Specialist and is the founder of Media Value Works and CEO at the MVW-MSME development center. She is based in Delhi/NCR and supports clients to grow business with integrated online marketing and can be reached at rachana@mediavalueworks.com)

Writing the foreword for this book indeed is an enchanting experience for me. It is not just because of my long association with Rinku and Amrinder but because it is about a topic that is so important in today's landscape. Over the last two years, a robust paradigm has witnessed digital transformation in overall business operations. And this is true for large organizations, MSMEs, and startups alike. However, the most significant afterthought for me, after an unrestrained 2020, 2021, is how Customers and individuals set the experiences in line with expectations. It catalyzed the paradigm shift as businesses continued to stretch and challenge themselves, and we witnessed the total transformation in overall business operations. Or maybe, in other words, digital transformation was the necessity to survive the blows of the pandemic and complete disruption affecting countries, businesses, and people alike.

Heading into 2022, I witness enterprises progressively embracing digital transformation to add a competitive edge to their business strategies. It is also helping with robust positioning in the antagonistic market. I believe Customer Experience with digital transformation was always on the agenda as organizations grew their size and scale and added more innovative features and capabilities to their arsenal. However, the pandemic accelerated the need and pace for businesses.

Simultaneously, from the consumers' aspect, I witness that they are gradually embracing technology. It brings ease and convenience to them. Even the government is bringing in more flexible regulations to enable greater technological adoption. It has paved the way for more extraordinary curated experiences for customers with technology as the enabler.

My two decades' experience working with various organizations has made a few revelations valid across organizations of different sizes and markets. First, customer experiences and mapping deliverables around expectations remain critical determinants of brand building to target customer loyalty for business growth with consistent preferences for self-service, personalization, and real-time resolutions. Second, this business growth, brand building, and digital transformation mean the people responsible for managing CX for their organizations must re-consider the consumer landscape and prioritize in new ways viz-a-viz changes in customer base and behavior over the past few years.

It won't be wrong if I say that Digital Customer Experience trends will likely gather steam as technology promises to address the challenges and opportunities for enterprises for sustainable growth. And taking customer needs and expectations will be the key to this development. Customers share information about their choices and viewpoints; they have expectations and problems, which becomes a necessary point of view even while designing the products and services. Creating customer-centric strategies is imperative for enterprises, and the inability to act on the feedback puts them on the back front. Lot many times, even when I have been working with different companies, this feedback aspect supported us with ideas for growth, engagement, and innovation.

The customer truly is king, so adopting the right approach to manage customer experiences has significant payoffs – for your customers and your bottom line. Customer Experience can give the brand the differentiation, innovation, and optimum usage of resources for profitability to create a viable and sustainable business amongst their competitor—the way of delivery matters over what is delivered.

The way enterprises engage with their customers directly affects sales figures, brand retention value, and differentiation from other brands as it caters to customer requirements by understanding customer behaviors. And this book precisely answers that for you. Every stage in a company, from idea generation to scaling it with processes, service, employee engagement, and governance plans, needs a systematic way to handle it. This handbook for the decision- makers certainly shall help introspect their customer experience journey.

As customers, we also know that our expectations are rising with the available knowledge and choices; hence, organizations have to fasten and align goals and objectives. And I must admit, as decision- makers, we often want a perspective on which initiatives to pick. For example, we think customer relationship management can be done by customer service, or we can manage growth without a strategic governance plan, measuring experience doesn't make a difference, or precisely we know our customer's journey. The book breaks the myth of the differences and why focusing on the right strategy for a problem can make a difference. I was enthralled that each chapter focused on one concept with plenty of examples to support it. So I can learn about governance by starting right from that chapter per my need. Each chapter is a new start to reflect on.

I just wish the readers a good reading time, and I truly hope this book supports the endeavor for the focused customer organization. It means more growth, innovation, brand building, and products/services that truly matter. You can build a 360-degree view of customers with the integrated data flow by understanding your customers and creating a customer journey map to develop an emotional connection of customers with your brand. And I should specifically talk about the impact of measurement, which is pivotal to tracking various metrics/KPIs to see the gap and growth with our initiatives to reach our goals. Metrics give numbers to specific vague interactions, behaviors, and deliverables and are more prominent as a multitude of data is created across multiple channels and customer journey touchpoints. The measures, frameworks, and concepts on CX can make a difference as you work to build a customer-centric organization.

I warmly congratulate the authors and welcome readers on reading, reflecting, and learning from the handbook to implement and create organizations that matter.

Rachana Chowdhary

(Ms. Rachana Chowdhary is the Global Media & Marketing Specialist and is the founder of Media Value Works and CEO at the MVW-MSME development center. She is based in Delhi/NCR and supports clients to grow business with integrated online marketing and can be reached at rachana@mediavalueworks.com)

Preface

"Building and Growing your Business through Customer Experience Management" is our venture to build and grow an organization/business through an approach of managing experiences for customers, both internal and external, including the end-users, stakeholders, vendors, etc. The book is compiled for you out of best practices, reflections from our consulting experience, fellow businesses, and research. This should help you succeed as a decision-maker irrespective of the role you play or the size and scale of your business. We aspire for this book to be your handy guide for various approaches you can undertake in your business by focusing on customers for growth, revenue, brand loyalty, and innovation.

Over the years we witnessed, the power and impact, entrepreneurship can create and the importance of engagement with various customers for innovation, sustainability, and creating win- win solutions. Solutions are built that alleviate nations pressing problems through and with customers.

We have practiced CXM through workshops, and consulting across industries and SME organizations. We have worked/interacted with Student Managers, Women Entrepreneurs, and Scale-up Enthusiasts in startups, Mid-tier organizations, Decision Makers, and Influencers.

To begin with, let us clarify what we mean by "Customer Experience Management" or CXM as discussed in the book. By definition, CXM is how customers engage with a company and brand, not just in a snapshot in time, but throughout the entire arc of being a customer utilizing the product/service for their need. It's a customer starting when he is contemplating their need for a product/service. At this point, they may use a search engine like "google" or talk to friends about a product/service or take references for a need. The customer experience for a business begins when a buyer is researching a need, evaluating a product/service and/or the provider for its purpose and usage or quality, pursuing and deciding a buy, until after-sales service. At every stage, when a customer interacts with a business, pulls some information, gives attention, or buys and experiences a product or service, a company gains more ground for its value addition. "Customer" must derive value from what the business delivers.

The famous Management Guru, Peter Drucker, says the work of the business is to create value for customers. In his words, "What the business thinks it is doing is really of little importance, because it is what customers determine as value, as important." In simple words, the value a customer derives can be different and is more important than what the business is creating. For example, a company might be selling a product to make digital transactions, but the value derived for the customer is the product's solution to their problem. In this case, it is the comfort of the accessible mode of payment anywhere, anytime.

Customer Experience Management (CXM) manages a seamless, engaging experience by providing quality products/services at the right prices per customer needs and expectations. You will agree that it is easier said than done. Through this book, we endeavor to highlight the practices of CXM which can be adopted in your business to build and grow.

For CXM, it is not just the marketing or sales whose work is to connect to the needs of the customer, but the entire organization has to be aligned. CXM is more than managing the experiences and the perceptions which customers are making for a company. It involves thoughtful management of providing value through products/services with constant iteration and improvement. Today, when time is a luxury, and the customers are spoiled with many choices, CXM is a strategy and a necessary tool for the focus to survive and thrive.

Basics are still the same for the business to provide value by connecting to customer emotions and expectations. In today's digital age, when disruptions are only constant, CXM is also getting more engaging and deeper through AI, machine learning, customer behavior data, and virtual reality for experiences that truly enhance the customer's value. These technology works are just the tools to create and define the experience needed. This advanced technology is for organizations already in a mature phase when they have interconnected systems for "One" engaged customer experience. SMEs, Startups, too can utilize these tools to create an experience, given the maturity of processes and financial stakes. This enables them to think above and beyond their products and services and bring in a customer perspective.

So, CXM necessarily is not static management of experience but a culmination of a dynamic set of experiences at various touch-points wherein the customer interacts with the organization. Today's time is also the age of GDPR when customer privacy matters and issues of trust matter. So, increasingly organizations with big pockets can falter in response many times compared to smaller organizations that engage with trust. Do you remember the time of the COVID lockdown in India, when all the big brands, the likes of Amazon, big basket faltered? Others stood up in these tough times like the *"Ghar ke pass wala Kiryana store"* (nearby grocery store) which managed to deliver these daily needs items to the doorstep. The storekeeper empathetically and patiently catered to all demands, personalized the interactions, and did not mind making multiple rounds to deliver. A lot of people formed deep connections and continued buying from these stores, maintaining their trust and association with the provider.

This brings essentially the objective of our book, and the CXM approach. Businesses need to connect to customer emotions and expectations to deliver value as per the need. It can bring differentiation by humanizing the entire experience, so the customer will keep coming back at the needed time and will bring their friends along. But mind you, herein, we are learning from all and most importantly from the large-scale organizations. We all are humans, so we will falter many times. The idea is to learn and get better and do what the business is set up for. In this book, we will share learning through the cases of big organizations like Amazon, Disney to further understand what CXM means to them.

We shall focus on understanding how CXM has been able to support its growth through an optimum investment of efforts and decisions to increase customer engagement, retention, and loyalty. It is business success through innovation, revenue gains, and brand loyalty. We will also look into many small and mid-tier organizations' cases, mainly from India, for more clarity and understanding of how CXM has been implemented and working for them.

In simple words, Customer Experience as a growth strategy implies

"HOW an organization delivers to customers is as important as WHAT it delivers to them. This is irrespective of its size, scale, or industry."

Over the years, we had the privilege of working with startups, women entrepreneurs, and many decision-makers across industries guiding them through their business plans keeping customers in the center, not only the end-users or clients but essentially the internal customers as well, in other words, the employees and partners or vendors. Driving success through customer experience management" is our trademark workshop which focuses on "What", "Why" and "How" of Customer Experience Management". Concepts from that workshop are explained in detail and embedded in the book along with our learnings from decades of practice in research, business transformations, strategy, consulting, and sustainability.

"Building and growing through CXM" is an honest attempt in providing perspective to student managers, entrepreneurs, and decision-makers as the world is opening up to creative approaches to managing businesses or clients and evolving rapidly. Some common questions we have listed below are the ones you may find yourself grappling with frequently while launching a new product, improving an existing product/service, or simply scaling up your business. You may want to understand,

- Is my product/service needed in the market?
- How do I make my customers stay with me in this intensely competitive market?
- How do I improve my product?
- How do I build a culture of innovation in my company?
- How can I enhance my customer loyalty?
- Is customer acquisition important? What should be the correct mix of customer acquisition and customer retention?
- Does personalization and how much of it support retaining a customer?
- How can I support my decision-making through my in-house data?

Above all, are customers always right? And does he always know? Should all the feedback be put succinctly into product and service? How, as a decision-maker, should I collect the feedback, utilize which metrics to improve performance, make decisions, and create strategy while keeping customers at the center of decision-making?

Hard questions are enough for creating a dilemma for every decision to be taken for the organization to move forward, innovate, bring efficiencies and make the best use of available resources, capabilities, and situations. Our effort through this book is to provide you with many answers and demonstrate how putting up the customers at the center of all decisions supports practical and optimum decision making. Engaging customers and focused value addition are sustainable for the business in the long run, as is for the short term.

Over the years, we have faced questions wherein we get a puzzled look from all followers, clients, and partners on how the CXM approach can be and should be integrated or is best accomplished for complete alignment in the organization.

We sincerely hope the book provides you with a lot of thoughts. In brief, the book shall highlight the

- Basics about Customer Experience Management
- Importance of Customer Experience Management for an Organization through Customer's Loyalty and Customer Advocacy.
- Best Practices and Tools/techniques for Customer Experience
- Measurement and metrics to design an engaged Customer Experience Management
- Changing dynamics of Customer Experience Management through digital and employee engagement
- Important components and strategy for an engaging Customer Experience Management Governance

For the ease of our readers, we have also used case studies in each chapter to better elaborate on the practical aspects. The cases are to reflect and implement CXM for building brand recognition, image, innovation, and loyalty.

We are excited, let's start building and growing through CXM!

Acknowledgements

We have been working together for many years. We started as a collaborator for a project and, over time, developed a lifetime friendship alongside our professional association. Passion for making a difference in the business landscape, and our camaraderie, made us start our company together. We offer consulting services and use our learnings, experiences, and skills to help our clients build their strategies around customer experience. Over the years, while working on the projects, we also enriched ourselves individually with projects in academics and coaching.

The book is the collection of our mutual learnings and the tools and frameworks we utilize to support customers, entrepreneurs, business leaders, students, and our associates. We extend our sincere thanks to everyone whom we have engaged with for work. Indeed, this would not have been possible if we hadn't had these chances to gather insights, understand, fine-tune and enhance our learnings.

We take this opportunity to extend our special thanks to Mrs. Preeti Tyagi, Mr. Atul Tyagi, Ms. Trang Hoang, and other fellow business owners whose case studies have been included in the book to enrich the readers with a perspective that comes from the real-world application of concepts discussed in the book.

Our heartfelt gratitude to our very first customer and now a friend, Ms. Rachana Chowdhary (CEO of Media Valueworks), for her unconditional support. She has been kind enough to grace this book with her Foreword. Our association with Ms. Rachana reminds us of beautiful words by Victoria Principal "When women work together, it's a bond unlike any other".

Customer focused approach is a game changer for an organization, especially in these times of rampant uncertainty. We sincerely hope this work adds to your knowledge repertoire. Human needs are simple but can be made complex by limited understanding; likewise, a customer-centric approach in organizations will need a focused intent and a solid understanding of the concept.

"Customer Centric" and focused organizations create products/ solutions positively impacting customers' lives and subsequently making the larger world a better place to be.

Last but not least, we are thankful to our families for their patience and motivation. Their candid feedback, honest reviews, and efforts ensured that we are aligned and need a mention for making a difference.

While it took a whole team of colleagues, family, and friends to complete this book, what is going to make this purposeful is when it finds its audience in you. We would like to take this opportunity to also thank all of you, our prospective readers, in advance and sincerely wish you find it useful.

Part1

Understanding Customer Experience Management

CHAPTER ONE

CUSTOMER EXPERIENCE – THE WHY AND THE WHAT

It's a world full of Choices

Every day in our life, we have numerous choices that define us to experience, learn and live life the way we want or desire. It contributes to our happiness, serenity, and well-being. "Whatever" is our choice, we bear the consequences and take necessary action if and when required. Certain choices work for us and, indeed, make us look at life from different angles. And we continue pruning our choices by getting more information if available and through our experience to lead an enriched life we want and in the way we want. There is predictability with surprise within our choices. And we will eliminate the choice that makes our life inefficient or anything, not up to our expectations and perceptions. Isn't it the same behavior with all of us?

Likewise, it is a perfectly competitive world in the business, too, where there are numerous options and choices to choose from for the same need. Same products or almost similar services for each Customer's needs and desires are present in every country across the globe. For instance, we can buy the same products at nearly the same price either from Amazon or Flipkart. Or maybe your favorite almost similar dress can be bought either from H&M, Wills lifestyle, or a local store replica. We are not arguing about the quality, just the presence of options for all of us. Even in heavy-duty automobiles, we can choose between a BMW and Mercedes or both or maybe Maruti and Santro's likes. Even if it's a truly innovative product for which there is a definite need, then there will be/can be versions for customer consumption. Apple is considered the best phone but it is not the only one, and there are likes of Samsung, one-plus, and various other phones for customer needs and choices.

The whole objective of all the choices talk is that the Customer is the king who makes a business whether currently, they are paying or not. With the advent of technology, numerous options, and offerings, customer expectations also have been enhanced. Customers are much more informed or maybe much more than organizations to make a thoughtful choice. They are now interacting, talking, and busy buying through different channels, resources, and devices for the products and services they need. And hence same way business is reflecting the trend of delivering value by connecting to customer emotions and expectations.

Regardless of their business, every company has to work hard in tune with the customers they want to serve. Customers choose a product/service from a business for the value they are getting, and if satisfied, they will return again and again and advocate the company to their friends and peers. It gives the business bandwidth to serve the Customer with more options, innovate, and continue the growth trajectory in normal times and during macro-economic disruptions like the pandemic.

We often come across the questions like, if the product has a good quality, the business shall thrive. We agree that the right price and quality as per the price range are non-negotiable in today's world full of choices. A company has to be sustainable economically for the long haul as-is for the short run. The business should keep having the old customers and continue attracting new customers, and it is true for a commodity or luxury products range for every segment and market.

Business and the Customers

Businesses thrive on customers and tirelessly work to add value or meaning to their lives through their products /services. When all the companies are offering the same value proposition in a given category, Customer Experience Management can give the brandthe differentiation it needs to survive the dynamically changing market! As we proceed we will know better how this approach could be a ground for innovation, and profitability, helping create a viable and sustainable business.

Customer Experience Management is a curated and informed approach that businesses take by defining experience at all interaction points as per customer expectations and perceptions. It is a differentiator that enhances customer loyalty and advocacy. Numerous types of research cite that most organizations cite and focus on approaches for utilizing Customer Experience as a differentiator. Because, a satisfied customer will be far more engaged with a brand/organization, as they will talk about the positive feelings and experience to family, and friends and will continue bringing in more customers along with their purchases.

Let's get back to how choices and preferences significantly impact the way we engage, focus, and work. In business, choices make or break a brand for a customer.Every choice a customer makes has so many reasons. And one of the significant ones is "How do they feel about the choice"? "How was their experience while buying, using, or interacting with a company "? Was it hard, was it smoother, was it memorable, and was it intuitive?

We human beings are necessarily not completely irrational, but our emotions drive our choices and this connects directly to the business market. Through curated customer experiences, businesses can create a unique value proposition and meet their goals in a fast-paced ever-changing market.

Numerous types of research prove that a satisfied customer is less sensitive to price fluctuations than an unsatisfied customer. And it is always easy to retain a customer than to attract and engage with new customers. So, when an online recommendation can make or break future sales, it is better to create a tribe of loyal customers. They talk about you, engage with you and buy from you to create a charter for growth and success. An engaging customer experience will create loyal customers and brand advocates.

Research across the world demonstrates that price becomes a lesser important factor when the customer experience is positive. Accordingly, 86% of people or end-consumers will prefer to stay with a company that focuses on customer experience management.

Customer Experience Management supports enhancing personalized connections with a customer by connecting to their emotions and expectations. It is valid for small businesses like a nursery, food, and education, as well as large companies, like manufacturing, etc. Every business serves the Customer, so building and growing through CXM can support organizations' vision and goals without any biases about how big or small the enterprises are

Figure-1.1: Customer Experience Management advantages for your business

Specifically, CXM supports building and growing a company as it brings better results in the following:

1. UNDERSTAND "CUSTOMER" for adding value

CXM and the tools such as feedback, customer journey maps, etc., can support a brand/organization in understanding how their product/service fulfills the customer's needs and quantify their attitude and preferences. We will discuss how these tools can be specifically used in business in the subsequent chapters.

CXM is a scientific and metric-driven procedure to understand customers and is a lot more than relying on gut feelings, past practices, or pseudo/incomplete procedures.

2.Enhancing growth and business success

Businesses have to make sure that they treat their customers well, or in other words, customers need to carry with them a positive emotion of their experience with the brand, for the business to grow and succeed. It doesn't matter to a customer that the business is catering to millions of customers at a time or has a series of processes to deal with contingencies. All that matters to them is a clear understanding/consistent experience that reduces their cognitive and physical loads or saves them time and effort.

In today's interconnected world, the customer decides the mode of contact with the business as per their convenience and preference. It is the customer who determines if the company is standing true to its brand promise and clearly how relevant it is for them. Aligning with customers' emotions and expectations is a work in progress and greatly supported by clear and consistent deliverables through process design, employee and environment-friendly policies, and intelligent use of technology.

3. Creating a tribe of loyal customers

Customer Satisfaction can enhance customer engagement. In today's times, the only way to survive when an online recommendation can break you is to create a tribe of loyal customers. They talk about you, engage with you, recommend, give pointers to improve, and buy/renew products/services to create a charter for growth and success.

Customer Experience through the entire journey will make sure that they are satisfied with becoming your loyal customers and becoming advocates because

"55% of people are willing to recommend a company due to outstanding service -- more so than product or price" (Stats from Superoffice.com. See notes for more details)

4. Greater clarity on where your organization is going and "why"

CXM uses numerous tools for governance, measurement, and improvement of processes, products, policies, and people. The tools such as customer maturity assessment, feedback processes like CSAT (customer satisfaction survey), NPS (Net Promoter Score), and customer effort score, help the organizational executive team understand and map their deliverables, strengths, and areas for improvement.

How things are happening, and why they are happening? This clarity on the existing working and execution in the organization is called the "As-is". This gives clarity to founders and the management team to understand where the organization is headed to.

CXM is as much about a business's brand promise for product/service pricing as it is about emotional connections while understanding the expectations and perceptions that a customer has for brands. It is much more about a journey on how Customers interact with a brand/organization which requires a reliable system, an engaged workforce, effective policies, and above all clarity about "Customer" needs, desires, and expectations.

"What" of Customer Experience

Daniel Kahneman's award-winning work "Thinking Fast and Slow" iterates that human beings by design are to choose the least resistant path as when working for a long time, humans hate cognitive effort. It is called the "law of least effort." Activities that are repeated get into an automotive mode through the conscious brain or the "System-1". The conscious brain works through a sense of familiarity with reduced efforts and energy to enhance pleasure. In simpler words, when CXM is applied to our strategies and workflows and put into practice, per the law of least effort, the employees will be attuned to the concept of "customer first". The idea is to provide greater experiences to customers with interactions that are seamless and personalized.

Converting this into the business sense is working on the "What" of Customer Experience" so that the Customer draws positive perceptions.

To understand the positive experience, consider the following pointers, Customer:

- should feel the interaction with the product/service is effortless
- should feel good about it, as it makes their life a little simpler with enhanced pleasure or efficiency.
- should match their expectations and sync with some earlier familiar good experiences through time and informed decisions.

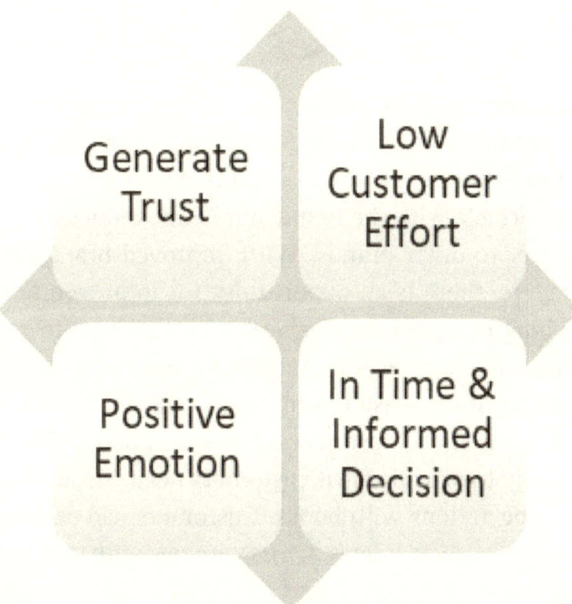

Figure 1.2: The ultimate objective of Customer Experience

Reflection

Have you ever noticed when you last visited a "Dunkin Donuts" outlet, a "Max" or "Life-style" store in the mall, or an online transaction through "ICICI Bank" in India, you are always asked, "How will you rate your recent transaction/purchase with us?" and "And your reason for giving the rating?"

It's an evaluation of the product/service providers of your assessment for them?

And did you give any rating last time? Do consider it. If your experience was good or ok, you should provide it, and if it is terrible it's your choice to give them the chance to serve you again or improve. Either way, your say matters

When the experience is effortless and in sync with the Customer's expectations, it enhances the "Positive Emotion" or the feel-good factor. The Customer thus gets into a mode of cognitive ease which leads to them getting more comfortable with the brand and hence reduces the chances of them switching over to other brands. With improved brand presence and trust amongst buyers, there is an opportunity for improved sales tracking through cross-selling or upselling. Businesses can step up to expand their horizon in the market and cover wider customer segments.

A classic example of this case is Amazon. It started from a small book store focusing on some niche customers. Jeff Bezos had a clear vision and deployed the strategy to provide what customers need. He kept giving value as per customer expectations with books. Customers had eased as they got books in the comfort of their homes across catalogs with good competitive prices. Customers stayed with the brand and Amazon kept on adding value and moved from this niche market to a multi-billion global organization. They worked with a primary focus on value addition by offering more products for the same customers, and slowly expanding to more target segments, making it a $386.064B company with a double- digit Y-O-Y growth every year. Amazon's growth story is when a small business grew by focusing on the customers they were serving and continuing on the path of value addition.

It's easier said than done to start executing by aligning your objectives around customer expectations and keep working on the same. Keeping a customer at the center of your decisions and executions forms the "What" and can be divided into five aspects of People, Product/Service, and Processes leading to Profits. These 4Ps include the basis of "what" of Customer Experience.

People

People include both the employees and customers. Customers are the pivot around whom the entire vision, planning, and strategy will come into play in the ideation, design, development, and prototyping of a product/service before being made available to them. Employees are an integral part because they are responsible to execute the company's objective and support the vision. There are many ways one can engage the workforce to drive CXM. Some of the pointers are listed below:

1. Employees, with their insights and customer understanding, can support ideation and prototyping decisions related to products/services.
2. With a better understanding of how their work impacts the end customers and the overall business results, employees feel valued and empowered to deliver on promises.
3. Involving customers at the start stage supports moderating a discussion on the problem that a product is trying to solve and its usability.

It is always better to invest both time and money at this stage in gathering insights to ensure that you have an offering that serves the right purpose and sets the right road map for your company.

It is only becoming more critical when one integrates customer experience from the beginning and does not wait until they onboard a certain number of customers. Understand, that the customer journey begins the moment you generate an idea, and hence the customer experience needs to be catered to right from the start. It is true at all stages if you are starting a new venture, developing an idea, or scaling the organization.

Five points to create a customer-centric culture

1. Clarity of objectives for alignment of customers.
2. Customer-centric objectives and statements to guide decision- making and efforts.
3. Focus on Communication across departments to make them work together, not in silos, towards a definite objective.
4. Knowledge sharing for informed decision-making and working.
5. Training and skill enhancement for upgrading and enhancing the quality of deliverables in sync with expectations.

Product/ Service

Product/service should be able to deliver value to customers as per their expectations. Products/services from different businesses have features depending on the usage and the value they are envisagedto deliver. The key to an adaptable product/service is design and quality control.

For instance, products/services might be personalized or customized, have settled features that fit the purpose, or have a certain sensory or visual appeal that makes them unique. The underlying phenomenon is product/ service should be able to deliver value and be more in line with expectations that have been communicated. For an organization at a starting stage or growing stage, it is essential to identify the target market and consider it in stages. Find out the early adopters for a product line, and they should be engaged from the beginning.

> *"If your business is successful with the masses, it must be successful with the early adopters... To be successful with the early adopters, you must sell them the why not the what – Simon Sinek"*

The law of diffusion of innovation describes how different sections of consumers can be identified and correlated with product life cycle stages.15-20% of consumers are innovators/adapters. These are the consumers who are always ready to try new things once they are convinced of the fact of what needs the product serves and why they should be using it. These are the influencers!

- 70-80% is the mass of the market who are the Majority and followers. They wait for the outcomes and performance of new products. These are the ones who do not stand in line for the first day first buy of a new apple phone. But the good thing is if we manage a good word with influencers in the market, this segment is not that difficult to buy. This is the section of our market that we plan to target in our growth stage: the full-blown launch!
- 30-20% remaining are the laggards whom we need not worry about. Any strategy could not work with them because the latecomers would probably not be very keen to invest in new ideas and are comfortable in their current state. They don't take risks.
- Bottom line is mainstream Customers are not ready for the product/ service in the initial stages of the life cycle, and we need influencers to prepare them to try the offering when building and growing our organization.

Use Customer Experience tools to discover the passion for your customers, and with a clear messaging strategy, find your early adopters and stand out!

Processes

The Process is set up of steps that convert the input into output and is joined by a feedback loop to improve and recalibrate for quality control and design considerations. The process gets important consideration in scaling up and at the startup stage because it becomes the initial step to develop the value addition to customers. It is a critical aspect of any curated experience that happens by design, with a great deal of understanding of the end-to-end customer lifecycle with the business. It involves the depth and details of how business is making its people across various departments work together to achieve a seamless, consistent experience to enhance positive emotion for the customer.

Five steps to creating processes that support CXM:

1. Processes should be defined at every stage (set of steps for consistency), so things that are giving results as per goals can be repeated, and errors could be minimized.
2. Governance through policy support and constant discipline to understand, measure, optimize, re-work, and improve processes per customer expectations.
3. A standard definition of customer experience should be created and managed for better clarity.
4. Integrate Customer Objectives with business objectives. It supports aligning the processes to broader business objectives.
5. SOPs (standard operating procedures) will bring uniformity in treatment and responses to customers and help create a consistent Omni channel experience.
6. Align or restructure different roles and processes for customer experience, translating to individual KPI and KRA.

The key is when starting; there is common knowledge available, so the chances of errors are a little less. But still, to maintain consistency and for better understanding, management must have processes that support CXM. It will also support growing stages when sheer side and numbers bring all the confusion leading to errors.

Key Takeaways for Decision-makers

- Customer Experience Management leads business success through greater customer engagement by understanding and tuning products or services to customer needs.
- When the experience is effortless and in sync with the Customer's expectations, it enhances the "Positive Emotion" or the feel-good factor reducing the chances of them switching over to other brands.
- People, process, and product/service are three indispensable parts of the customer experience

Notes

15

CHAPTER TWO

DYNAMICS OF CUSTOMER EXPERIENCE MANAGEMENT (CXM) ACROSS INDUSTRIES

Customers don't want to hear about product features, benefits, or even solutions. They just want outcomes. They just want the job done - Simon Mulcahy, Chief innovation officer at salesforce.

Every industry, every organization, irrespective of its scale, is in the business of serving its customers. Serving customers is a value- addition through the organization's product or services as per customers' needs and expectations. Now, "Needs" seems to be an essential connotation for business existence. When understanding "Needs," we will realize it will have different annotations for different people but for our purpose of understanding needs that drive buying behavior, it's the "wants" that shape the choices for meeting the so-called "Needs." It is an understanding of the famous Maslow's theory of motivation based on human beings' "Needs." The theory contemplates that human beings have basic survival needs and these move from basic survival needs to something that adds purpose and happiness to life. For example, we need food to survive. And our wants decide what we will eat, which depends on our liking, availability, and/or any other benefit we seek from food.

Even if we go by a standard definition for business, "Needs" are the attributes of a product or service that the customer buys. The same phenomenon will have different needs for different people. For example, an exercise regimen offered by a fitness center will cater to the different needs or should we say wants of different people. In this particular scenario, the need of all buyers is fitness but the choice of a particular regimen is driven by the specific want, it could mean losing weight for one person, or looking attractive for another. The same need leads to different choices culminating in different wants.

Different people can have different needs for a product which can be attitudinal, psychological, or behavioral. As per needs and expectations, organizations create, innovate and serve customers through their products and services.

Understanding the needs of customers is easier said than done and requires a tremendous amount of work on the part of the organization. It has to continuously learn, engage, update, and innovate to continue adding value for customers. For instance, consider a simple customer service support request for a failed payment transaction. It will need deep dive by the executive through some basic and minimal questions, a good knowledge of the bank's policy framework, decision-making ability, and empowerment to take appropriate action and solve the particular problem. If tackled well, this transaction has the potential of providing customer satisfaction and ultimately making it a delightful experience. What needs to be highlighted is that it calls for tremendous back-end work in designing the processes and continuous improvement on the part of organizations to make the whole interaction more meaningful and effortless for customers.

Every effort of personalization and customization of products and services must also consider following along with customer's expectations:

- How much should a company cater to?
- Will it fit its business model?
- What would be the correct and ideal way?

Now we understand how customers' needs are somehow influence by their wants. A concept developed by Harvard professor **Clayton Christensen** helps in understanding it better. It is called "Jobs to be done". The idea follows the logic that a customer gets a product or service to get a job done in their life. The choice makes their life more comfortable or accessible. So, it means getting into customers' shoes entirely and seeing why they make certain choices and what drives their decisions is critical to knowing what serves them best. This idea of customer perspective or outside-in view of customer experience management is all about and has been in the works for some decades.

Let us look at another example. A team was working to see how to enhance the sales of milkshakes in a fast-food delivery chain. Despite a lot of efforts, nothing substantial came out. A research scholar sat the whole day to understand and observe customer behavior at the fast-food outlet. He observed that the sales were more in the morning hours, as people bought shakes to kill the boring commute time and give them something substantial before the next meal. This led the team to create thick milkshakes with a straw that could be held in one hand while driving. Rest the milkshakes can't always be thick and were of different consistency and flavor basis the needs influenced the wants of the customers.

"Jobs to be done" is an excellent way to understand needs influenced by customers' wants. After a good product and service market fit, an organization must work to deliver on promises with full attention to added value.

People, processes, and technology can make a difference in the product/ service. Like for an organization of a fast-food outlet with stores worldwide, the quality and timing of the service become important even if the product is standardized. Localization and customization can always add extra flavor. However, the deliverables matched with brand value can make a difference. The other case could be boutique firms like flower shops that can create customized experiences through personal connections. Insummary, people, processes, products, and technology all stitched together create an amazing experience for the end user. This starts with identifying the customer's expectations.

Consider another scenario. Imagine, if the customer service executive asked you endless questions verifying all the information. The executive then connects you to another senior because the issue can't be resolved at their level by repeating the same or more such questions. Maybe the issue was not resolved, and instead, you were given a timeline for hearing back from them. What will be your reaction? Are you already beaming with frustration?

It does happen and is a case with many organizations where the customer has difficulty finding timely solutions to their problems. And it is not only with startups or substantial scale organizations but with organizations that focus less on the customer and on continuous improvement to enhance the experience. And in the world of choices, when the customer feels he is not valued enough, they shift. It is a perfectly competitive world with multiple options and choices available for every product; service and customer retention are getting trickier, thus needing focus.

The awareness of "time and attention is a luxury not everyone can afford in current fast-paced times" while serving a customer can help design engaging experiences.

People Centricity for CXM

Customer Experience Management practices are more people- centric, with people being the internal employees or external stakeholders and end-users. When built with people at the center, effortless experience with all processes and technology brings an optimal investment of effort and money.

CXM practices and tools are sector agnostic and the focus for CXM is to understand the customer and then backtrack to create the experience and enhance customer engagement, internal and external. Customer Experience Management focuses on customers and tries to be as attentive as possible by tracking, overseeing, and organizing customer interactions. However, with the ideology being the same the methods of work change with different cultures and countries, and industries [1]. It is mainly because different cultures have other belief systems. Therefore, customer experience management practices need to be built with context for a country, sector, or industry by understanding the ecosystem it operates in and not just the customers. This goes without saying that aligning the brand promise with deliverables that match customer expectations still forms the center of the entire CXM effort. Customers in today's time interact with an organization through multiple channels, including digital media and physical stores across industries. This calls for an approach that is thoughtful, in-depth, and holistic to address all the variations that each channel would bring with it, as far as customer expectations and market dynamics are concerned.

The practices are built on core principles, including expectation matching as per the brand promise, enhancing ease by innovating, and aligning the entire organization to deliver consistent performance and hence elevated experience. In the end brand promise, and aligning it to customer needs and expectations is the core.

Let us now go through a couple of case studies to elaborate on the point of "Customer Experience Management" across industries. We start with cases of two giant companies who have been pioneers in adopting the "Customer Experience Management" practices from around the globe. Then we go further with two mini-cases of adoption of CXM in education and a designer startup to draw and build the understanding. The whole idea is to understand and develop how startups or multi-billion companies deliver value while keeping the customer at the center.

Integrated Approach of CXM a case study of "Amazon"

Case 1

Amazon – The Scale and Size built with a focus on Customer Experience

Amazon.com – the name we reckon and one of the world'svaluable organizations collected around **$26.9 billion** (from April 2020 to March 31st, 2021) in profit and operate in major economies worldwide. The company sells everything from books to jewelry to digital music and is a significant player in cloud computing with the development and provision of services in 'the cloud.'

Amazon is truly a leader compared with its competitors, and the revenues/profits have increased consistently over the years since its inception in the mid-nineties.

Amazon has changed since it started over the years and has an embedded vision to become truly a 'customer-centric company. So, what began as the goal to become the world's biggest and best online bookstore developed into a store where customers could buy "anything while the company and its execution focused on customer-centricity

Amazon's founder, Jeff Bezos, is a pioneer who started focusing on delivering value to the customer right from the start of his venture. He has built the company purely, focusing on Customers, which earlier was an empty chair, and now Customer Experience Bar Raisers. With passion, Jeff Bezos focused on the unbending, unyielding philosophy of serving customers across all departments.

Summarizing Amazon's Customer Centricity broadly, as following

1. Customer-Focused Culture

Right from the starting days of Amazon in the late nineties, Bezos worked to create value for the customer. It didn't just become a vision but an overall philosophy and strategy to build the business. It didn't matter who the customer was; the focus always was on customers from top to bottom hierarchies in the organization.

Amazon's vision is "to be earth's most customer-centric company; to build a place where people can come to find and discover anything they might want to buy online." It meant a razor-sharp focus on customer needs and quantification of the impact on Customers due to various company decisions.

Thus, Bezos always set his meetings' tone with "the empty chair." Bezos bought an empty chair into discussions early on so the decision-makers could think about how their decisions and policies affected the outcome for the invisible person or the customer. Over time, it has been replaced by "Customer Experience Bar Raisers," who influence decisions at all levels in the organization. The customer could have been invisible, but the unmistakable presence of the customer is always accounted for.

2. Understanding Customer Needs and Aligning Company's Deliverables around it

We're not competitors obsessed; we're customer obsessed. So, we start with the customer's needs, and we work backward." This is the philosophy.

For instance, at Amazon - the Kindle tablet and app used for easy access to reading came into existence purely for customers' needs. Storing piles of books and costs could become an essential differentiation that enhances customer efforts. And hence, the need and customer obsession led to solutions that we use today, and it became a pioneer for a start to all digital content. We say customer obsessions lead to innovation. The Kindle tablet is the perfect example of it. It took many R&D efforts to recognize customer problems, including reading strain and creating an ecosystem to make the readily read books easily available. The Kindle tablet and other apps were born due to customer desires and needs and not becoming an engineer's preference. One case repeatedly discussed is when Bezos was questioned about the cost of building a Kindle as it took many years. He was asked how much will he spend on this project, and Bezos promptly replied: "How much do we have?"

3. Building and Working to maintain the Customer Trust

We are the digital age customers. It means we research heavily before trusting any product or service. We check the digital medium, talk with our colleagues and friends, and even post and read about complaints online. You will agree that we as a customer may know more about options and substitutes available for the needed product and service in many instances. Organizations and even respected brands have mishandled situations, and getting and managing the trust holds the key to Customers sticking to the brands. It is not about not making a mistake but acknowledging, accepting, and taking necessary steps to ensure the customer is treated with respect. This philosophy of honesty, integrity, and effort will make a difference for the customer. Be it a multimillion company or a startup which has just started building its avenues.

Amazon has a razor-sharp focus on customer experience. Over the years, technology, ease of user experience, and customer service have created a leading example for others to emulate. And Amazon also had its share of controversies. For instance, back in 2009, there was significant controversy about Amazon's behavior without user consent. Amazon had remotely deleted copies of certain books from its customer's profiles. The books were "1984" and "Animal Farm". This incident created a huge cry and backlash from its customers as Amazon tried controlling and dictating the choices of customers. And the incident meant that Bezos himself acknowledged and apologized for the incident after their initial apology or dry press statement didn't stir any emotions. But when Bezos worked to connect with its customers by taking full responsibility, it turned the tide in favor, and the customers forgot the incident.

For the incident, Jeff Bezos wrote that "Our 'solution' to the problem was stupid, thoughtless, and painfully out of line with our principles," he said. "It is wholly self-inflicted, and we deserve the criticism we've received. We will use the scar tissue from this painful mistake to help make better decisions going forward, ones that match our mission."

The books that were removed were pirated; however, the founder's acceptance and communication helped restore the faith, wherein many customers commented and thanked Bezos.A heartfelt apology accurately represents acknowledging and creating a path that an organization cares about the customer's needs. This connection can work more than any advertising or marketing gimmicks.

4. Constantly evaluating the Customer Experience to Improve

Never Settle for 99%

""We're not satisfied until it's 100%.""

This focus to keep improving and keep seeing to make things better was instrumental in building the company which Amazon is today. Jeff Bezos focuses on audacious goals, which pushes the company to improve its deliverables. As the technology of barcodes, IOT worked to improve the efficiency of deliverables to the level that a package put in the wrong truck too will send a warning to the concerned employee. Amazon, very early in 2000, created a system through technology that only four packages were misplaced in 4 million (A Six Sigma Accomplishment). It has been taken completely today by app-based solutions with complete tracking of packages, deliveries, and routes.

Amazon Management works not to enhance the costs to reach a benchmark price to maintain customer trust. Still, the focus is to protect fragile and delicate customer trust, leading to long-term customer retention and advocacy issues. Minimum queries asked for product return issues and prioritizing to focus on projects help Amazon come closer to its customer.

Today it is all digital, and thus it becomes extremely important as customers are talking to one another and are referring to companies that provide a more satisfactory customer experience.

5. Each Customer is valuable and should be connected with as is Amazon

Organizations should aim to connect to each customer using data and technology to build a genuinely lasting company.

A Forbes contributor Jonathan Salem Baskin has an interesting story to share. (Source: Forbes.com)

As per the author, he got a letter from Amazon informing him that the price of his books had dropped. Of course, the price advantage the customer was getting was a small one. But the gesture made the customer loyal to Amazon.

More so, the customers get accustomed to Amazon because of the price advantage as the absence of intermediaries makes the retailer pass on the benefit to the customer. But also due to the deliverables which suggest more options basis the preference of other customers and the customer's behavior. Customers can get trust by also reading about other people's experiences with the product. The advantage of intuitive service makes all the difference to the customer not to switch to other competitors. Because convenience does matter, at last, it builds the habit of engaging with a brand repeatedly. Testimonials like these add to an organization's revenue building.

Amazon is a truly customer-centric company as its departments are entirely data-driven based upon the success and failures of the customer experience. It allows them to take risks to innovate and make difficult decisions because the teams work to understand and distinguish different customers to create solutions that work for the customer. Ultimately, if a customer is happy and satisfied, it leads to a more profitable company. Amazon works to connect to each customer through its user experience and technology. The endeavor is to provide solutions that exceed customer expectations.

Case 2

Disney - Changing dynamics through employee engagement and digital experience

Disney's theme parks worldwide focus on bringing families together to bring huge smiles through experiences filled with memories and fun.

Disney theme parks have longevity as Customer Experience leaders and are one of the "Most Valuable Brands in the World." Reported to be worth more than $28.1 Billion, the House of Mouse is raking up profits consistently from the previous year.

Disney's story started 50 years ago when celebrated filmmaker Walt Disney created a concept by dreaming of another kind of family experience that engages and celebrates. In Walt Disney's words, he wanted a place where families could experience an atmosphere of detailing embedded with rich storytelling. Thus, over the years, Disney has created an approach through deliverables and experience to exceed its customers' expectations. And the most surprising part of the customer experience is the 70% return rate for first-time Disney visitors.

If we get into detail, we may find that Disney's approach to its deliverables, and the magic it creates, is through a focus on the process of creating extraordinary from the regular. It means it works with the support of ever-engaged teams and employees, and technology. Walt was obsessed with the process, so he encompassed and worked with employees and technology to develop methods that produced delight and entertainment. He believed that the backbone of Quality Service was built on designing perfect processes and then repeating them at scale.

Disney has seemingly held to these process-focused beliefs by giving close attention to the details and continuously improving the process. Disney and his teams, since the start, focused on four keys in everything they do. The employees are trained in these concepts. For Disney, the four keys are Safety, Courtesy, Show ready all the time, and efficiency.

Some examples mentioned in *Be Our Guest-A book by Disney* include:

1. Figuring out and fixing the gaps in experience

At Disney, it was observed that despite regular and consistent information on the required height to enter a ride, the young child would often weigh with their parents only to find out that they aren't tall enough. The team found that it was a major complaint, and obviously, kids and parents didn't feel good about it. To compensate and convert this low point, the management empowered the employees. It worked by creating a special pass for the kid to skip the lines on their next fun ride at Disney.

2. Caring for every detail, including the parking

The Disney team worked to ensure a smooth, convenient, and pleasant end journey as had been the experience in the park. Magic extended even for the exit of customers from the park as well. The team at Disney figured out that their guests had a problem finding their cars in parking when leaving on trams. They found a solution by creating a process for the "Tram owners" in the parking lot to keep a simple list of rows they worked on that morning. This information was then distributed to all the team members by the end of the day. It allowed that when guests came back, the tram drivers knew which location the car was parked in and guided them to reach their respective vehicles. Ending an experience in a convenient and caring manner went a long way to ensuring satisfaction for the guests.

3. Employees are the internal customers to create value for the company

Employees build the company, and Walt Disney believed in this concept firmly. He realized that creating processes and innovation meant that the employees had to get better every day at what they had been doing. So early on, a lot of focus went personally into resources. For instance, in 1931, if a person had been a young animator taking classes in Chouinard Art Institute in LA, then at times, even Walt Disney could have dropped in as a chauffeur to the animator and the other group for classes. The desire to learn was focused much on the company. Later even the lead teacher was hired from the institute to support the employees, reducing the need for employees to travel. Walt worked while believing the concept that finding the right people and giving them the resources they needed was the only way for him to accomplish his dream. Together with the right team and efforts combined, an organization achieves its goals.

4. *Empowered and Self-Sufficient Team*

Walt Disney had been focused on the process constantly. However, he also recognized the importance of building empowered teams that could function and make decisions independently. This focus made many innovations from the ground staff at Disney. Walt didn't create the strictest paradigm for the team, but in a simple sense, it had been more of talented people with shared skills and learnings working together. The processes had been built, so the team was self-sufficient to work with minimum commands. The teams were dedicated, and Walt Disney ensured that instead of minimum errors or maximum efficiency, he needed a team that could make the greatest creative effort. It is believed that Walt Disney was even ahead of time, and if output mattered, he could even have set up a remote work kind of system. He focused on the best output with the best people available.

5. *Interconnected teams in touch with Customers always*

In the early years of the company, the focus always had been that the employees should mingle with the customers tofind ways to make the experience enjoyable for them. Sitting at office desks was avoided by design. It was explicit learning and mandate from Walt Disney himself. The focus on cross- collaboration meant that even the company executive didn't operate in a silo or bubble and cross collaborations supported the innovation at Disney.

For example, the customer research team found that the guests had trouble understanding certain characters. The team worked to create a smoother process for the customers by fixing the places or greeting locations to assess different characters and sharing the information with signs, pamphlets, and the CHIP (Character Hotline and Information Program). CHIP resulted in phone numbers and connectivity to clearly understand where different characters are. It leads to lesser crowding and more individual connections.

Technology, too, is a part of the magic wand that Disney is wielding in their experience for the future. With a bit of pixie dust and a lot of Bibbity-

Bobbity-Boo, they work mainly with the aid of technology to transform the experience for its guests to remove some of the frustrations (long lines, no seats at the show, etc.) that can mar the park experience for guests.

Disney also has an exploratory team called the Next Generation Experience project. Focusing on creating "more immersive, more seamless, and more personal experiences for every guest," the group has four goals namely, driving operational efficiency, transforming the customer experience, personalization through connected products, and enhancing interactivity across channels.

Disney employs analytics to streamline back-house operations and improve labor resources as needed over time."Magic Band"; or wristband in the mail that will contain the customer's personalized itinerary in its snug, tiny confines. With the Magic Band on their wrist, they can have the whole experience of Disney World with a wave of their hand, or in other words, like magic. They can arrive at the show with just 30 seconds to spare and still have a seat. They can bypass the lines at your favorite rides because you have a preselected time to ride them. They can also buy food, drinks, souvenirs, and merchandise with a wave of theirhand, as the band will be linked to their credit card. My Magic+ was designed to allow customers to customize their itinerary at the park. The customized itinerary means plans as per their need, desire, and wishes. The customers can book rides, plan shows or make restaurant bookings. The application is customized to interact at regular times with the customer to remind them, and it is done in real time to create an enjoyable holistic experience. For example, the new experience works like this. Guests buy their tickets online. Then the customers can plan and customize their day as per their wish. Then they can choose which shows they want to see, the rides they want to take, and how and where the food will be consumed. Experience at their own pace and desire.

Technology was worked and accepted early in Disney to create holistic experiences by understanding customer behavior and preferences. The Magic Bands are part of a new "vacation management system" which monitors consumer behavior and their buying journey preferences to support real-time data to the team to create more customized and personalized touchpoints and experiences for its customers. Even the traditional Disney stores with trademark merchandise have app-based experience involving technology through kiosks for interactive, 3D navigation and search. In addition, the Disney store has connected systems for video clips, articles, and social media feeds.

When they see that the popularity of their parks is starting to hurt the experience, they focus on creating a convenient, smoother way for user experience. Disney's success is in its focus on creating a Customer Experience culture and Employee Engagement. Having your employees buy into your brand promise and live up to it every day is integral to a great customer experience.

Case:3

WOW kids

The third case is about a company that is working in the education sector in the preschool category.

"Wow, Kids" is a preschool based in India which boasts innovative pedagogy, experiential learning, and engagement with franchise owners and parents all over India.It was born out of a passion for working for children's holistic and complete development to help them face future challenges in 2014. It is co-founded by Mrs.Preeti Tyagi and Mr. Atul Tyagi.

"Wow, kids" is doing exceptionally well with franchises all over the country. They hit a bump in the road during the 2020 COVID lockdown in the country. During this time, the firm's focus and practice of customer experience management supported the tide over the extreme disruption.

Interestingly, "WOW kids" franchisees are all over India and are run 95-98% by Women. Users are young kids aged 2 to 6 years, and parents are influencers and key stakeholders. The biggest challenge in the lockdown for the company was to keep functioning, engaging with franchise owners, training, and updating the curriculum in a way that it becomes easy not only for kids but also for parents and teachers. Online education needed focus and commitment with a complete understanding of the stakeholder's needs and expectations.

Covid-19-induced lockdowns affected the education sector the most. The education sector had to adapt quickly to continue delivering value while also taking care of its users who needed a different type of engagement with both physical and psychological aspects of learning. The biggest challenge had been about what, when, and how to teach kids from 3 to 5 years of age. At such a young age, parents were not willing to take risks. They had an option to take a break from studies too. So, the signups were mostly on hold at the start of lockdown in 2020. It needed creative measures while adopting the technology.

The franchise partners also had a difficult time in business due to depleting cash flows and no further clarity on the way forward with Covid restrictions.

The "Wow" management team assessed their current situation and put up a strategy in four words to survive this. Engaging, adapting, innovating, and communicating. They focused on these four aspects for practices to keep the ball rolling. There were challenges in the adoption of technology, curriculum, and apprehensions from parents. The focus had been on transforming negative emotions and thoughts into positive emotions. Numerous heart-to-heart conversations supported the transition to online education, where the infrastructure and training had to be done quickly. Online programs were started with focused efforts after understanding parents' preferences and users' needs.Numerous steps were also taken to tide the disruption by engaging with partners. Franchises were mentored and guided for cash flow to take care of significant expenses. Management Teams were optimized for working.

> *"Our communication has grown and beyond with partners since the Covid lockdown situation. If anyone wants to grow in business, customer service and experience should be unforgettable, and then they become brand ambassadors" – Atul Tyagi.*

Customer experience and connection to consumers is such a significant collaboration and empathy to survive the tough times. Customer Experience so that customer needs are understood and deliverables are transformed to create winning scenarios.

It also supported the "Wow" to innovate with more solutions. They have put together early childhood global classes through the Facebook community. New solutions and paradigms are emerging with early childhood educators. A single platform for sharing ideas is piloting new solutions and ways to transform education into a complete experience. The company is growing and adding value to all its stakeholders.

Case 4:

Customer Experience Management for a "Designing Studio"

Customer Experience Management holds tremendous significance for a niche segment like Interior Designing studio dabbling in consulting and designing projects for housing and hotel segments. It's a case of an interior designer based in Vietnam who specializes in Vietnam-based lacquer art and has clients with various residential projects and hotels.

Ms. Trang Hoang, by profession, is an interior designer based in Vietnam. She picks projects with various hotels and housing segments and has high client referral rates because she specializes in Vietnamese art and has unique art-based designing approaches. Clients were happy. However, she realized over the years that her engagement with clients and her team issues made her waste a lot of energy on trivial things. Here she wanted to enhance her art, imagination, and designing skills; on the other hand, running a business needed a personalized approach to support her work. She was also losing some client referrals, and managing the business was overwhelming. Because in the end, her design studio needed a business approach for the greater satisfaction of all stakeholders while achieving the client's objectives.

"Customer Experience Management" supported her to balance the focus between business objectives and enhancing the design skills of designers.

How did CEM support the Designing Studio?

Per Ms. Trang Hoang, she and her team created processes to understand their customer more personally. They worked to understand their customer preferences, choices, and thought processes and thus developed plans to improve their customer's experience, thus increasing their satisfaction and loyalty.

A design studio needs more personalized approaches because the key to creating a " Wow" experience is to understand customer behavior, choices, and emotions. In addition, for a design studio, the customers vary in age, outlook, and objectives. And thus, flexibility in approach supports personalization.

So even after designing, the team picked construction projects that needed collaboration with many players; most of the time, the clients left the onus with Ms. Trang's design studio. And the team worked to create a seamless, consistent way of doing work by adopting customer-focused processes in their way of work.

Some ways adopted by Ms. Trang and the team -

1. **Pre-project information** - Ms. Trang and the team have created some personalized, structured surveys to understand the needs, requirements, and choices of their customers beforehand. The surveys and pre-project information supported understanding customers' expectations for the designing studio and paved the way for client expectation management and trust-building. Professionally yet personalized project management goes a long way in smooth functioning and attaining objectives for the designing firm and the client.

2. **Processes with role clarity for employees** - Though Ms. Trang's design studio has a very dedicated and focused team of designers. However, managing and delivering work as per deadlines became a minor hurdle. In design work, deadlines for various aspects can get trickier as it involves a lot of creative work and imagination, which can hamper the settled target deadlines.

Understanding customers' expectations and aligning the stakeholders as needed has supported Ms. Trang's deal with some contingencies. It's a work in progress. However, the clarity has started sinking in and will get better as they move with time.

The outcome of the CEM initiatives

As per Ms. Trang, the focus on enhancing customers' experience has been tremendous in their services and business. The profits are enhanced through more referrals and conversions. Smoother and consistent functioning has improved customer satisfaction both for internal customers (employees) and external customers (the various stakeholders and clients). As per Ms. Trang - " the focus has improved our services with a high rate of returning customers. New contracts are signed quickly, and it is also helping us to reach more new customers. She concludes that "Customer Experience Management is a strategic process which is needed in every brand. As long as you still have or want to have customers."

Key Takeaways for Decision-makers

- People, products, processes, and technology aid in creating engaging experiences.
- Customer Experience means creating entire organizational deliverables with customer expectations that are fueled by their needs and wants
- People can make a difference in creating a personalized and customized customer experience as the framework can be laid by organizational policies guided by the communicated brand value.
- Irrespective of the organization's size, which can be a multi- billion-dollar company or a small boutique firm, organizations are in the business of serving the customers to support them to get specific "Jobs to be done."

Notes

CUSTOMER EXPERIENCE, CUSTOMER SERVICE, AND CUSTOMER RELATIONSHIP MANAGEMENT - THE PARADOX

"Success is not delivering a feature, it is learning how to solve the customer's problem" Eric Ries

There has been a dilemma in the mind of decision-makers/founders! Despite the numbers reflecting excellent Customer Service and highly satisfying Customer Relationship Management, Customer Experience Management is still not moving up the metrics chart.

How come implementing Customer Relationship Management software or putting up an elaborate team and processes for customer service is not sufficient for an enhanced experience for customers?

In this chapter, we explain how Customer Relationship Management, Customer Service, and Customer Experience Management are different pillars of a larger network of top-line customer experience management.

Customer Relationship Management, as the name suggests works for the simple goal of managing relationships and engaging. Technology is the enabler for the management so that the whole relationship management is effortless and smoother for the current and potential customers.

A CRM system from technology providers works to streamline processes and procedures to help companies stay connected to their customers to work on the deliverables, awareness, and engagement initiatives. A CRM system can track the sales funnel right when the company starts engaging with the customer with relevant contentor creating awareness about the product or service to close the deal. Even after-sales connections with customers for loyalty and references can be touched upon using a CRM system. Various CRM configurations are available in the market, including enterprise-level to cloud-based solutions for companies of different sizes.

On the other hand, customer service is a streamlined methodology to provide support, assistance, and advice when using a product or service of a company. It is necessarily a part of the complete experience that a company offers to its customer, which supports it in retaining its customers and getting many more. In the words of Tony Hsieh

"Customer service shouldn't just be a department. It should be the entire company".A customer service agent represents the entire organization in the service to the customers. They talk about the organization's culture, brand, and focus, and thus selling your product directly or indirectly.A well-trained, empowered customer service agent can not only enhance your brand value and customer loyalty and maybe it can create more upsell and cross-sell opportunities

Let's try to understand more nuanced differences between customer experience, customer relationship management, and customer service on a broader aspect for clarity and adoption in our businesses through the comparison below,

	Customer Experience Management	Customer Relationship Management	Customer Service
What it is about	It is a perception customer carries for the deliverables in line with their expectations at every touchpoint across the entire journey It leads to a holistic perception of how and if the business deliverables are meeting the customer's needs	With the help of technology, businesses interact with potential and current customers engagingly.	Provides customers with a point of contact for the company and is usually through interacting directly at the store or by phone w h an employee/staff.
Nature of Interaction	It is the holistic feeling that customer holds from different channels and at all interaction points and keeps him loyal to the service/product.	Transactional as various information is analyzed for supporting organizational decision making to support customer decision making	Is transactional and provides an opportunity to deliver excellent customer service by being friendly and helpful.
Customer Behavior Understanding	CX is about understanding your customer so well that you can predict customer behaviors and expectations and deliver a basic all-around view of the customers.	It is mostly about supporting customer behavior patterns by mapping different purchasing and other behavior to support organizational decision-making by providing to-the-point deliverables as per need.	Customer service most commonly is related to the contact that helps you record your problem and provide for resolving it.
Nature of Approach by the Company	This is a proactive approach.	It is proactive and reactive	Reactive in nature. Though is an important part of business

Customer Experience Management prioritizes customer relationships and creates frameworks and processes for delivering value. Customer service further acts as a point of contact to support customer queries and challenges during and after purchase points.

CXM helps tie all the threads, from different functions like CRM, Customer Service, Sales, Marketing, Human Resources, Purchase,and others, to provide the ultimate experience for customers. It calls for the entire organization to work as a single unit and work on a common goal of keeping the customers first.

Customer service earlier was considered a cost center. However, it can be a source of competitive advantage in today's time. For instance, consider a healthcare firm that sells high-value products. Though by design, the product doesn't need much support, in case it does need it, the company which provides it naturally will get customer preference. Customer Service, Customer relationship management are most definitely a source of customer satisfaction but not the entire foundation of customer experience management.

Reflection

Customer Service can enhance the usage and overall product experience. And for this, the company does not need a presence in every corner of the world and country.

Consider the case of homegrown (India-based) and bootstrapped unicorn "Zoho." The company has multiple business products, including CRM, marketing, invoice management, and analytics. Designed and customized specially for small and medium business needs. The unique model of Zoho involves robust "Customer Service" using technology. Its agents connect very easily through online chat support and are fully trained to support the customers.

Robust "Customer Service" enhanced Zoho's product adaptability and thus the company's success when they had a fierce competition to deal with technology giants.

Customer Service can have unique models created as per the target customers' needs with the simple intent to support them.

Curating and optimizing Customer Experience and Customer Service with Relationship management

With supporting technological solutions, customer relationship management can provide insights into customer behavior, preferences, and feedback to learn and improve. Customer Service too can provide several inputs on product usage, service lacks customer pain points, and other opportunities to improve the overall experience. It can enhance collaboration across departments.

Find below a few recommendations when **implementing customer service and CRM solutions** in your company

- In Customer Service, a long-term perspective and solutions to create an omnichannel engagement can create a holistic, connected service across channels.
- Trained and empowered employees who can take decisions to support customer-centricity or customer focus. The primary input is that employees need training, empowerment policy support, and a clear understanding of the organization's brand value. It will support them in taking necessary actions to enhance customer engagement. For example, a customer connects to a company to seek support on using a company's service. If self-help channels are not considered sufficient by the customer, then the agents need to be trained to listen and respond so that the customer feels connected. A positive experience from customer interaction with a customer service representative, so the customer hopes that there is a way to solve the complaint. Someone is there to support.
- It is not about the speed of solving the problems in Customer Service but how the experience has been for the customer. If the problem hasn't been rectified, the service team ensures a complete redressal of the same through later connect. It will ensure customer satisfaction. They would like to engage with the company again. For this, an organization will need feedback, processes, and policy for creating empowered internal customers.

CRM solutions

CRM solutions as of now are mainly used to support sales. However, CRM solutions also help experience by maintaining a relationship with customers through communication. Even customer service can have insights to support customer cases and improve journeys at all touchpoints.

- Understanding the need to implement a CRM solution can go a long way to defining which and how it can support desired results.
- Mapping out the organizational processes will make the implementation and further usage to aid decision making.
- Consider scalability and ability of CRM to be integrated with other technological solutions in the organization like the ERP systems
- Training support and the ability to migrate data from one platform or CRM to say social media tools can be vital to utilize the data generated through CRM to create value for customers.

We can understand this paradox further through the case study further.

Case

Customer Experience Management (CXM) with the aid of Technology, Service, and Relationship management

This case is on an indigenous healthcare provider in India, Cloudnine Group of Hospitals.Cloudnine Group of hospitals focuses on maternal and childcare, and a visionary management team undertakes this specialized niche under the leadership of Dr. Kishore Kumar - the current Chairman.

Customer Experience has been an intrinsic part of Cloudnine hospitals, supporting its growth and scaling across the nation and other geographies. Technology has been the enabler for this focused, digitally empowered niche. In the company, the experience started with the aim of continuous improvement to create a Wow and cherished memories for customers as putting in the words of the chairman Dr. Kishore "aim to *Wow*" them and to give them an enjoyable and memorable experience. This is our guiding principle in all our decisions,".

Hence, the chain of hospitals has resorted to engagement with their customers across the complete journey. It involves communicating about the services and programs to the expectant mothers, introducing them to the team of specialists, keeping expecting mothers updated with upcoming milestones, reminders, etc., along with post-delivery care including consultation, childcare, and vaccination schedules through the "It's our baby" app. The Cloudnine hospitals are building an ecosystem through the application by collaborating with other service providers to provide one-stop niche solutions for parenting, healthcare of Moms, online consultations, door-to-door medicine delivery, neonatal units, and so forth. In addition, Customer Relationship Management through digital communication supports the engagement for a superb overall experience for customers.

Even the hospitals have worked to enhance customer service by using digital enablers. This involves logging in every customer query and using a simple process for faster turnaround times. Also, regular scrutiny of gaps for improvement has been a way to enhance deliverable standards. "Voice of Customer" and "metrics like "Net Promoter Score" have been driving the actions and decisions at Cloudnine hospitals to build a culture where every stakeholder and employee believes their contribution in the impact it is bringing in for its customers.

It is growing at 35 -40% CAGR (Compounded Annual Growth Rate) with reported 430 crore revenue in 2019 (19% jump over last year) as per the previous reports available.

The pandemic only supported the organization's efforts for more engagement for its customers. It has created a community for Moms and an e-commerce store for in-house deliveries and consultations through the platform. Customer experience has driven the organization from its inception to scaling.

Key Takeaways for decision-makers

- Customer Experience means keeping the "Customer at the center of decisions." Effectively it means serving by building a relationship by supporting and adding value to the customer.
- Every employee of an organization is in the customer service department as they embody an organization's brand value and culture.
- Optimizing customer experience will need relationship management and customer service to provide data and insights across the customer's journey for measures to improve and provide deliverables as per the brand value.

Notes

Part 2

Customer Success through CXM

CHAPTER FOUR

UNDERSTANDING CUSTOMER SUCCESS

"Customer success is not about support. It's not about being reactive. -- It's about being proactive." -- Guy Nirpaz

Having understood what Customer Experience means and all that we need to imply from the term Customer Experience Management, it is time to get deeper into Customer Success and how customer experience management helps you deliver your best!

It is quite common to use Customer Success in our business discussions. After all, any business that exists thrives on the accolades of its customers. However, you would agree that Customer Success is a very subjective term, and what it means to any organization could be very relative to its specific vision, targets, or industry.It is not a metric or a strategy element that can be applied without knowing what it truly stands for. In most organizations, it is the function that is held accountable to manage the relationships with the customers.

The goal of the customer success team is to address escalated situations or be a point of contact for clients to reach out for any clarifications, questions, or concerns they may have. While the customer is at ease to see someone dedicated to them and feel valued, the organization's leadership considers this as a medium of drawing an unbiased view of the client. There is no doubt the effort is made to make the customer feel valued and special under the assumption that it will strengthen the relationship with customers and in turn, be an aid to recurring business or reduce the possibility of losing customers to a competitor. It's an evolving function and hence is interchangeably used with customer relationship management. The function is mainly set up outside of sales or engineering/product teams.

Also, when we use the term Customer Success, it primarily refers to external customers i.e., the client base, and comes with an added cost. If not organized well with clear communication of roles and responsibilities, this may lead to more problems like internal conflicts or confusion for the customer, besides impacting the bottom line.

When we use the term "Customer Success" in the context of Customer Experience Management, it is not used to refer to a particular function or a department. It is used to address the holistic association with the client. The focus is not just on one aspect i.e., customer relationship, the emphasis is on ensuring that the customer takes away the maximum returns from their investment in a product or service. The systems are integrated and processes are set up so that the enterprise proactively works on client engagement. The perspective here is to see success for a client in the true sense. It is to understand the value and experience that the client is taking away with it on any and every transaction. It is not to be treated as a mere improvement in metrics like customer retention or customer engagement but to ensure that the organization is a true collaborator with its client and is working to align its offerings with the client's agenda and motives.

Amazon is a great example to share and help dig deeper into the concept of customer success. As Jeff Bezos, the CEO of Amazon quotes "We see our customers as guests invited to a party, and we are the hosts". The customer strategy is based on three drivers mainly, stellar buying experience, time-sensitive delivery, and 24x7 customer support. When one thinks from the customer successlens, it's a great place for shoppers to find most of their needs, compare various products, track the history of their purchases, make a purchase, and/or return the item sitting at home, etc. The brand has surpassed all expectations of online shoppers or retailers.

Often Customer Success and Customer experience management are also confused as being the same; however, it is not the case. To understand this better, let us use an analogy of a building. Consider Customer Experience Management as the foundation on which the various building blocks stand. In this particular case, building blocks could be Customer Success, Feedback Systems, CRM, Metrics, Measures, etc.

The Customer Experience focuses on a holistic view of clients associated with a brand and their positive experiences at different interaction points. Leading from CX goals and intentions, Customer Success works to create opportunities for customers to extract the most value from the investment. The insights most often lead to product engineering and betterment of features to improve usage, fitment, training support, etc. The main drive for the customer success team is to maximize the extent of the solution to the client's needs through the product/service.

Customer success is more visible in product companies or B2B companies. These companies follow a more proactive approach. A lot of energy goes into adding value to the product for customers. and building insights to achieve customer success. This would help enterprises find opportunities for recurring revenue, renewals, and cross-selling. Customer Success in the B2B environment is about return on investment, knowing customers enough to keep adding value. Experience, however, is more prevalent with every transaction that happens for all purchases by a customer. Whatever the differences or similarities may be in the two concepts, the important thing to take away is that both the concepts are working with a shared intention of returning value to customers and continually improving on it.

Reflection

Customer success teams benefit small organizations as well as large- scale or multi-national companies. However, the point to note is that the customer success approach is relative and dependent on multiple factors like the product or the solutions, the customer base the organization is catering to, and different functions. Whatsoever,

- The team must be clear of its roles, responsibilities, and the goals to be achieved. Most of all, the understanding is that their presence is crucial for organizations' success and that their contributions can bring a positive difference to customer experience.
- Agility in operations, understanding of the importance of KPI and metrics, and the awareness of goals are needed to establish standardization and also instill the idea of experimentation.

Look out for the change-makers or "Customer Success" team in your organization!

One could argue that a business should focus on its outcomes and goals and it is an overkill to think about customers' goals. What if we just focus on delivering what we need to deliver and leave the client to make its choice? These are valid arguments and worth consideration. It may all sound very confusing but all we need to consider is that we do not ignore the customer's point of view in any decisions we take as an organization and ensure that we make outside-in perspective a part of culture and habit.

We can put some blame for this confusion and also on some myths/ stereotypes about customer success. Here are a few stereotypes associated with Customer Success as a function or goal that you must be cautious of when working in the role or setting up this function:

Stereotype #1 Client Retained is Customer Success Attained

Broadly speaking, this is the most common misunderstanding we carry around being successful in attaining customer success. Often, we believe that if the customer is with us for a long time and uses our product or services, it would imply they are loyal and will continue to stay for time to come. These are often the clients who are susceptible to topping our priority charts but still neglected.

It is very important that before we conclude on a client like that, we must acknowledge the fact that is it possible they are continuing with the offerings only because they don't have much of a choice; they are stuck with the product for a long and moving to another would call for more investment and change or just sticking to you because they are too busy handling their own business and essentially adding overheads to manage extended issues.

Be careful not to imply the basis of the longevity of the client to be successful with that client. It is possible anytime soon, with changed leadership and more options in the market, they could just shift their loyalties from one to another supplier. This happens in a lot of cases wherein a client that shows green suddenly quits the company!

So, solidify assessment about client lifetime with details on their experience score, engagement level, repeat orders or usage of the number of services in your portfolio, or the span of impacted employees.

Stereotype #2 24x7 Customer Support = Customer Success

As in other aspects of life, in business too, we as humans have this knack of twisting any philosophy into something convenient to us or molding it into our way of approaching. Customer Success also has fallen into this pit for a long time. Very commonly Customer Success is confused with Customer Service in a significantlywrong way. Customer Service is more reactive than proactive.

The whole purpose of the service desk is to record, keep all the issues and ensure they are closed on time within TAT. When we look at Customer Success, the purpose is to make sure we are proactively looking at possible concerns or discomfort of a client in a given situation or instance and work towards the larger aim of improving clients' overall experience—knowing them enough to know what problems we can solve for them with our offerings. Excellent Customer service is just one aspect of a larger bucket of customer success. 24x7 support through various channels for clients to report their queries or issues isn't serving the purpose if we are not looking at repetition of similar issues, same client reporting issues frequently; how are communications being handled and recorded, consistency across channels and so many more that we will address in future chapters

Stereotype #3 More sales imply Customer Success

Like any other metrics, we can very easily be misguided by our sales numbers to draw an inference on our customer success. As business owners, we have to be very careful of looking at the big picture rather than thriving on pure numbers.

Understandably, sales have their job and targets on their heads to meet. In today's scenario, it is only becoming difficult for teams to meet their revenue targets. What we cannot also deny is that there is a large population of professionals who are using legacy sales concepts and pursuing hard-selling, making unrealistic promises, and in a way misleading clients with a single purpose of making a sale.

In today's market dynamics, legacy methods do not apply. As a business, we can only survive if we sell by listening more than telling. What this would mean is that one has to keep looking for any concerns or problems in the conversations with prospects. Staying alert to the clients when they share, being authentic and transparent, and at the same time being empathetic goes a long way in building their trust.What we do want to make sure of is that we are not only looking at the short-term transactions from the prospects but making long-term associations basis trust and transparency.

Stereotype #4 Saying YES to Customers is a sure-shot way to Customer Success

Keeping Customers first is the most misunderstood concept that we as consultants have noticed. Being customer-centric is never leading to saying yes to everything that customer says.

When we say that we need to be customer-obsessed and keep them first, it is never to consider them as a king or God! Let us just understand there is hardly any customer success achieved by putting clients on a pedestal that dehumanizes them or makes them unapproachable. They are humans first and there must be some ground rules to how we plan to engage with them. The most critical aspect of any client engagement or customer success plan is that it firmly aligns with the organization's offerings and most importantly its values and vision!

Keeping the customer first and hence moving towards customer success is all about being able to have an outside-in approach wherein we ensure we have mechanisms in place to know our target segment, understand their behavior and expectations, and be aware of aligning our products/services and our goals around this understanding of our target audience.

It most definitely doesn't mean saying yes to every demand but making sure we are honest and transparent about what we can and what we may not be able to solve for them. The art is in communicating assertively and empathetically and delivering on promises that we make!

Stereotype #5 Customer Success Manager (CSM) per client ratio is a key

Sometimes the whole business world makes us so mechanical that we end up following the books blindly without considering our own specific unique business needs. We have observed that irrespective of the size and scale of organizations we end up setting up an organizational structure that optically suits trends or justifies our resources. When setting up a customer success function we have seen so many myths coming to play that it is almost frustrating to watch as a consultant.

The biggest myth that one goes with is that there is this defined model for customer success and certain ratios should suffice to decide the number of resources. Needless to say, this impacts the operating costs in hiring, training, and many other associated allocations of funds.

Having a customer success manager with no clarity of how and when the function needs to come into play with the client may lead to confusion at the customer's end as also growing internal conflicts. Keep in mind sales, pre-sales, customer service, and others also have a role to play directly or indirectly with customers.

So, know that there is no one size fits all approach for setting up a customer success function. As a decision-maker one has to be aware of specific client situations, prioritizing clients that may need more attention and have a higher impact and/or the span of the client. It is possible that from the long list of clients, there are a few that are manageable without CSM and/or may need one or even more than one CSM aligned to it. The objective is to clearly articulate the purpose and objectives of what one would like to achieve with this role and then communicate effectively with concerned parties. Any overlap must be handled and not left unattended.

To wrap this up we must know that at all times the only key differentiator for us to thrive and survive in business is stellar customer experience management ultimately leading to customer success. Be it a startup or a mature organization; brands must look at implementing customer success via customer experience management. Keeping customer sensitivity at the center of any strategy definition is critical to their growth. Specifically for startups, there is an opportunity to make a strong start by implementing both Inside-out and Outside-in views for their product or service offering strategies and actions.

Explicitly talking about startups in the SaaS model, wherein most brands spend their resources on marketing and sales, must rethink fund distribution and look at customer success as a good investment. Since the survival for these setups is on subscriptions, focusing on sales and enrolling new customers is often considered critical. A better long-term strategy to sustain and thrive in the market would be to figure out ways and means to maintain the subscriptions through renewals and referrals.

Implementing Customer success doesn't always mean making considerable changes in the system; one could start small and gradually mature into the process.

In the next chapter, we will focus on finding what customer success strategy can be used as a framework for unique needs. The key is always to understand that Customer Experience Management is the underlying factor in building this strategy.

Key Takeaways for decision-makers

- The goal of the customer success team is to work proactively to avoid escalated situations and manage client interest at all times and be available for any clarifications, questions, or concerns they may have.
- Customer Experience is more about focusing on a holistic view of clients associated with a brand, and their positive experience at different interaction points. Leading from CX goals and intentions, Customer Success works to create opportunities for customers to extract the most value from the investment.

Notes:

CHAPTER FIVE

STRATEGY FOR CUSTOMER SUCCESS

"A satisfied Customer is the best business strategy of all."
– Michael LeBoeuf

An eagle eye on what your customers are experiencing with your brand is eventually going to define how successful and confident they feel about their decision of choosing you to serve their needs.

It may appear that mere focus on customer experience management would eventually lead to customer success, but this is not an accurate interpretation. Designing and implementing a customer experience strategy would increase the probability of customers feeling satisfied and happy about the engagement, however, to ensure your brand is also an active contributor to the client's success parameters, one must consider defining a clear and actionable customer success strategy.

Devising an impactful and robust Customer Success Strategy is simplified and depicted in the figure ahead,

Figure- 5.1: Customer Success Strategy

Let us understand what the MCP strategy implies. This strategy can be applied with the following three pillars:

Being Meaningful

It implies that our vision and our goals must be in alignment with our customer's vision and goals. As a brand, we cannot afford to lose sight of how we are adding value to our customer's personal or business goals.Consumer behavior has changed dramatically in recent times. Today a buying decision is not just driven by the need, it is about adding meaning to one's life, it is about creating an identity, and serving a purpose and hence it is even more critical for a brand to be attentive to these aspects.

Here is a quick checklist for you to know how meaningful has been your offering:

- Are your business ethics and values aligned with those of your customers?
- Is your business vision and goal aligned to that of your customer?

- Is your collection of data relevant to your business objectives and customers?
- Are the insights you are drawing and communicating directing to any meaningful outcomes for your customer?
- How are you ensuring your employees are finding their daily work meaningful? Do you align with their purpose?

Being Customer-Centric

Keeping customers first can be very challenging to implement. An organization is required to imbibe the concept as a part of the culture to the extent of obsession with fulfilling customers' expectations and needs and providing for them over and beyond.

There is no easy way to go about building a customer-centric culture. It requires awareness across the organization andconsistent effort to create sensitivity within the system. The goal here is that it comes naturally to every employee, stakeholder, process, or system. There are a few cautions to consider when deploying customer- centricity or customer-first within the organization. Keeping the customer first implies that you treat customers like God or putthem on a pedestal that caters to any unreasonable demands or a culture of never saying "No" to them. The idea is to ensure every decision is vetted for customer impact and to be empathetic towards them.

A few pointers to build customer centricity are listed below:

- Is there a consistent and correct understanding of customer behavior and triggers or their needs and wants across the board?
- Is there empathy towards the customer in all interactions and demonstrated in actions?
- Is leadership taking the right steps to communicate and train employees or stakeholders on customer sensitivity?
- What checks and control measures are in place to ensure that the customer is the center of all decisions and actions?

Being Proactive

Today to stand out in the market, a brand has to speed up its reach and actions to customers. This in no way means just delivering the product on the agreed end time, rather, it is about how proactively you act on every aspect of your customer dealing. A small miss could cost you a customer.

Again, on changing consumer behavior, the expectation is to receive your product or service in the shortest time and most often a complete update on the buy status.

Therefore, proactiveness is not just limited to delivery or after-sales but has to be maintained throughout the customer's journey.

There are many technological advancements like digital solutions using big data, Artificial Intelligence, or machine language to predict customer traits and brands working their product, marketing, or sales strategy around those analytics.

If you are a proactive organization, you must be looking at the following key elements:

- How proactively you are communicating your company, product, or service updates to your stakeholders?
- Are you proactively reaching out to your customers and listening to what they have to say about their experience with your brand?
- Are you proactive in collecting predictive data and developing your future strategies and actions around these insights?
- Are you proactively devising strategies to engage your customer and empower them with their decision-making?
- Are you watchful for changing trends and patterns in consumer behavior?

To summarize, a reliable customer success strategy is to stay **Meaningful**, **Customer-Centric**, and **Proactive (MCP)** as an organization in all your decisions and actions. It may look complicated initially, but once it becomes a part of your culture, it promises amazing returns to you as a business where your customers are happy and want to stick to your brand forever!

Never forget your key bottom lines to a stellar customer success strategy:

- Invest in time and other resources to build a solid understanding of your customer behavior, triggers for their buying decisions, needs, and expectations. A simple tool like Customer Journey Map can come in very handy to achieve a 360-degree view of the customer along with strong modes of recording their feedback and experiences.
- Leadership commitment goes a long way in making any strategy work and delivering its promises. Leadership must create an environment that is tolerant, creative, and transparent for it to allow everyone in the organization to consistently work towards the assigned mission and put words into real actions.
- Be aware of the fact that customer engagement and employee engagement go hand in hand. If the employees are feeling valued and find meaning in their daily work there is no reason why they wouldn't be motivated to deliver the best to their customers. So, keeping employees' aspirations and goals aligned with the company's goals and objectives is very important.

To further add to your thoughts about Customer Success Strategy and its implication for your business, here are simple but real case studies of a couple of organizations that implemented customer success strategies to achieve the desired results.

Case

Customer Success Strategy in Product Company Industry:

Learning and Publishing

Product: Digital Learning Solutions for Personal Growth and Development (Inspired by a real case our team worked on)

Implementing Customer Success Strategy to Enhance Customer Experience

Introduction

This company is a start-up and owns a digital learning product with a wide range of topics leading to individual personal growth. The courses follow a strict framework and undergo scrutiny for plagiarism and the quality of content. These are short-term courses in the format of a classroom wherein the subject matter experts address their specific topic in a recorded video with worksheets and assessment tests.

Given the challenge of many such providers of online content, a few leading brands for that matter, the customer was looking to increase their client base and also gather reliable constructive feedback to improve their product.

Choosing Customer Experience to stand out in the market and make steady and steep growth in the industry was the step in the right direction. After the intense market study, product assessment, and analysis of current customer experience management maturity level, setting up a customer success strategy was the chosen path.

Needless to say, after a year of focused effort on customer success and implementation actions the customer gained a 4% increase in sales revenue and a customer engagement score of 4

The Story of the "Product Company"

This company was set up with a mission of providing quality online courses on key skills and competencies that an individual needs to stay employable. The target audience was job seekers, freshers, and mid-career professionals specifically who were looking to grow in their profession or readjust their career choices.With this niche, the content was also very specific and oriented toward the current needs of employers and also future demands. Content providers have to register for Empanelment and go through a rigorous background check and experience validation process.

The biggest competition was leading online course providers offering similar courses within an affordable range of price and also easily accessible.

The Challenge/Opportunity the Company Faced

This enterprise made entry into the market with some good prelaunch and launching programs and had a very impressive beginning. Over the last three years, they managed beta programs and made significant improvements to their product making it more stable.

With a good start to their credit and maintaining a loyal customer base, the customer was keen to take proactive measures and ensure continuous growth in client acquisition as well as look for customizable and more flexible learning opportunities for clients to meet their individual needs.

The opportunities and challenges that they were looking to overcome were,

-Stand out in the online course provider market with customizable learning opportunities

- Continue to penetrate the retail market as well as explore B2B opportunities
- Learning is an ongoing process and customers wanted to make sure their clients keep coming back to them for any future needs hence customer engagement was critical

Why did they choose a Customer Success strategy?

This is a fairly young start-up and for it to grow and be successful in its business goals, it was the need of the hour to stay informed on how its users are engaging with the product and capture their experiences. The product serves the personal growth need of their clients and hence it was all the more imperative to build their trust with the brand to build a strong customer relationship.

Through due diligence on existing systems and processes, there came a quick realization that while the brand has strong customer support in place that is performing very well on response time but it was still catering to the problems at hand. The focus of customer support was more reactive and towards one specific problem for a particular customer at a time.

So, the question that needed an answer was, how to integrate a holistic view of Customer experience with the product and the brand as a whole.

The customer Success strategy was one strong and reliable way to achieve positive results. The only way for the brand to be successful in its set goals was to see its customers achieve success

Recommendations and Steps taken

As stated the intent was set with the team to infuse the organization's vision and business strategy with customer success ideology and identify ways and means to work around it.It was envisaged that this would require a multidimensional approach so that the approach is effective and sustainable.

The following steps were taken to make this happen:

- Reintroduce and communicate revised organization vision and goals to the team.

- The Customer support team was restructured as the Customer Success team with the objective of:

a. Issue Resolution
b. Empowered team well trained on customer sensitivity
c. Proactive and personalized communication at all times so that customer feels valued and special at all times
d. Install systems to enable self-help documentation or troubleshooting sources easily accessible and available reducing their effort on the usage of product or understanding. Chatbots, FAQs, and digital user manuals were some of the immediate investments.
e. A dedicated resource team to engage with customers was set up to interact regularly and gather insights on product experience like usage, impact on personal success, learning experience or quality, future needs, etc.

With the passionate team at the helm and committed leadership to back it up, this was a successful program that resulted in a strong loyal customer base

Results Achieved

- Increase in Customer Retention rate: 4%
- NPS Score of 24
- Customer Engagement Score of 4 on a scale of 15

In the end, the brand was making steady progress and penetrating the market with a niche segment of keen learners looking to upgrade themselves and prepare for better career opportunities.

Customer obsession leads to innovation, this is an underlying principle of all customer experience management organizations. Customer success would be an important pillar of innovation as it aids in establishing the ecosystem to not only collect new ideas but also builds tolerance to evaluate and implement in the best interest of the organization. It is interesting to know that innovation and customer success go two ways. Innovation may not necessarily always be an idea introducing something very new but it could be a simple idea that helps do the same actions in a more refined way.

Solution-based mindset and value creation are two of the key traits that lead to new and big ideas. Business leaders must work to build an environment within the organization that encourages people to fearlessly share their minds on new and creative ways of addressing customer problems and adding value to existing solutions. This culture of innovation is amplified if the enterprise can include consumers themselves in the process and allow them to lead to a better tomorrow.

One of the greatest living analogies that explain how customer success and innovation are so intricately tied together is the live streaming OTT platforms, Netflix being the leader followed by many others

It led to the disruption in the entertainment industry with the latest emerging technology intervention with its cloud hosting, using AI or big data for streaming the best of the content that is personalized, suggestive, and infinite choices made available, even offline, for its subscribers. Customers are empowered today to choose how and where they want to spend their time.

Customer success is an assured enabler to customer- obsessed innovative culture within an organization by being meaningful, proactive, and customer-centric. Another important element to this would be an engaged workforce that feels empowered and valued enough to deliver over and beyond their expected job responsibilities.

This leads us to the next logical step of understanding how employee engagement is critical to customer success strategy.

Key takeaways for decision-makers

- Customer data and information and expertise to use it for breakthroughs is key to customer success
- Include customers in the value creation process without overwhelming them
- Innovation breeds customer success and vice versa
- Starting small with trial and error can help manage transitions better
- Being watchful and quick adaptation to emerging trends is the magic formula for customer success
- Be authentic and stay true to serving customers and solving their problems

---

Notes

79

CHAPTER SIX

EMPLOYEE ENGAGEMENT FOR CUSTOMER SUCCESS

"When people are financially invested, they want a return. When people are emotionally invested, they want to contribute." Simon Sinek

There is no denying the fact that manpower is the most critical resource when it comes to customer success. Our staff engages in transactions daily that impact customers directly or indirectly and hence we cannot ignore the fact that our employee's experience is directly proportional to our customer experience.

So let us explore and address some of the critical questions that will help us boost our Customer Success and hence accomplish enhanced customer experience.

- What is Employee Experience?
- How does it impact Customer Success Strategy?
- What are some practical approaches to Employee Experience?

Understanding Employee Experience (Ex)

Ex is a perception that an employee draws throughout the journey, at every interaction point, with the organization. In a global value chain that serves the client, every employee plays a crucial role in driving business through efficiencies. Employee interests and values need to be Aligned with the enterprise's vision and goals. Company policies and decisions must integrate employee experience parameters throughout the process chain, from the front to the back.

Organizations often take employees, their internal customers, for granted. The majority of resources and energy are focused on the end customer. This could be detrimental to an organization's success story in long run.

The need of the hour is to focus on employee engagement with one single objective and that is to **"Boost Customer Success by driving Exceptional Employee Experience"**.

As a first step to enhancing Employee Experience, one needs to have a strong grip on understanding employee wants, expectations, behaviors, and emotional needs or triggers. When it comes to deploying a reliable Employee Experience strategy, it is not a linear effort, rather, it follows a multidimensional approach. As laid out in the diagram below, the following are the three dimensions of Employee Engagement.

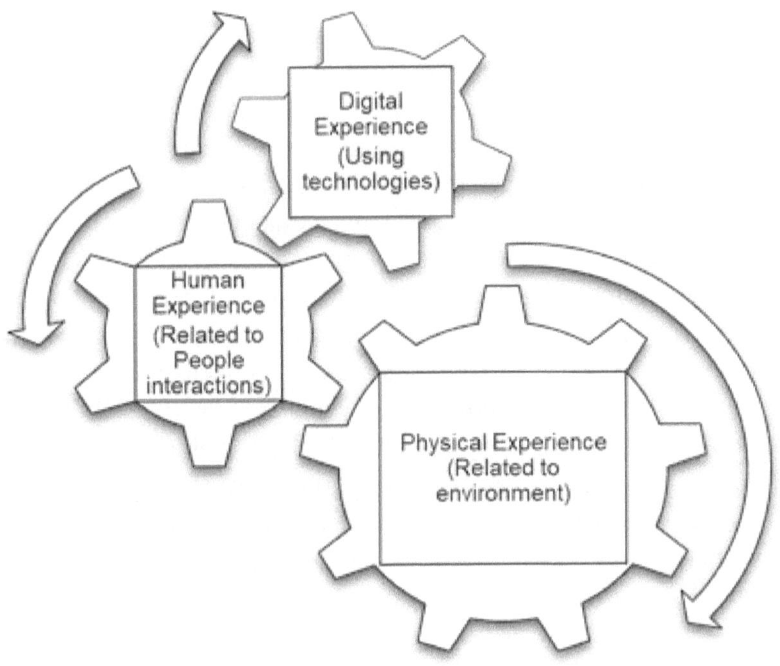

Figure 6.1: Three dimensions to Employee Engagement

If as a brand you are looking, to begin enhancing your employee experience, you must know that the program covers three typical aspects:

1. Human Experience which is more directed towards the human interactions that your staff is experiencing. This would include any interaction involving a customer, other employees or managers, vendors, or any other stakeholder for that matter. Do the employees feel empowered or do they feel restricted to a documented process and hardline instructions?

2. Digital Experience derived from systems; technologies they are using to make their job more impactful. It is important to know if the technologies are making them more effective and efficient in their work or if it is slowing them down. As an organization what efforts you are

making to handhold their transition from manual work to automatic work? Do they look at digital transformation as a threat or an opportunity?

3. Physical Experience i.e., related to the work environment, be it safety and security of staff, cultural aspects, work ethics, and values. Is the environment in the organization motivating for your employees to come and deliver their best every day? What kind of employee behavior is your environment encouraging? Are the employees feeling respected? Is the environment and company culture encouraging new ideas?

Every organization may need to look within and understand where their efforts need to be focused and how each dimension is playing out for the success of employees leading to the ultimate success of customers.

The important thing is to ensure we have clarity in what we want to achieve and hence it becomes equally critical to define objective goals. One can begin outlining their goals as per underlined figure that highlights 4 buckets of key outcomes that any and every employee experience effort must consider:

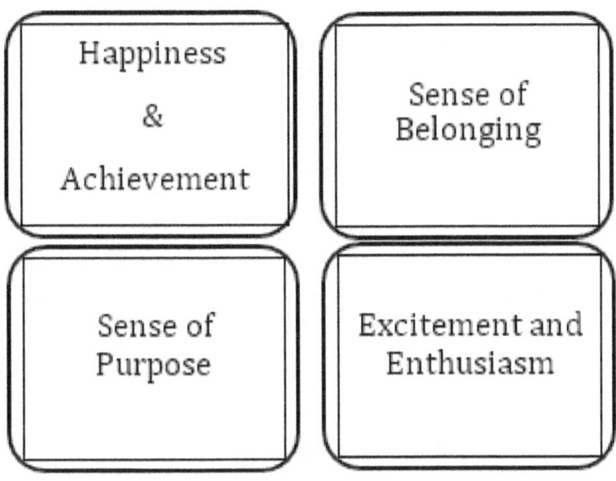

Figure 6.2: 4 Key Outcomes of Employee Experience

As a brand, it becomes imperative to offer happiness, a sense of achievement, sense of purpose, belongingness, excitement, and enthusiasm to its employees.

Leadership, including business leaders and Human Resources, must come together and devise ways and means of inspiring and energizing their workforce towards higher performance and greater wellbeing.

Reflection

Feeling respected and trusted at the workplace are significant motivators to create an engaged employee culture. Worldwide, people prefer and have highlighted that respect from their leaders is important leadership behavior to them.

Even mutual trust between people leads to a lesser focus on issues, and the emotional energy which is limited thus, is spent on things that matter

Respect and trust at the workplace need curated Employee Engagement strategies and focus!

Engaged employees lead to engaged customers!

While it is not impossible to work on the strategy, there are some challenges that as a company one must be aware of. The few generic ones are listed here:

- Majority of the workforce today is increasingly shifting to Millennials. The triggers for this section of generation are quite different and hence expected to change the employee and employer dynamics.
- Employees are expecting not only productive and engaging work but also an enjoyable work experience that adds meaning to their lives. It is no more about just salary.
- Attracting and retaining the right talent continues to be a challenge as the expectation and behaviors are shifting at a very high pace. There is more exposure and opportunities are global.
- Lot of organizations still consider Employee experience or engagement as a function limited to HR

There is a need to reinvent our approach to the whole employee engagement effort. Some of the approaches that would come as aid are:

- Focus on an integrated employee experience as compared to the legacy approach of employee engagement initiatives running in silos or specific departments.
- Design Ex with clarity on the kind of workforce to hire and retain, one that fits perfectly into the company culture and value system.
- Shift focus from the needs and wants of an employer to a more balanced approach where the employee expectations align with the organization's purpose and mission.

An employee Experience strategy that focuses on greater employee sensitivity and culture transformation is the one that will lead an organization to a successful outcome of Happy employees and happy customers.

Excellent-EX is about understanding and providing options that enable them to deliver their best every day, to their fullestpotential, and be equal partners in driving business value.It requires building customized experiences based on different employee segments or also referred to as employee personas.

In a nutshell, a simplified approach to implementing Employee Experience is wholesome as explained in the diagram below:

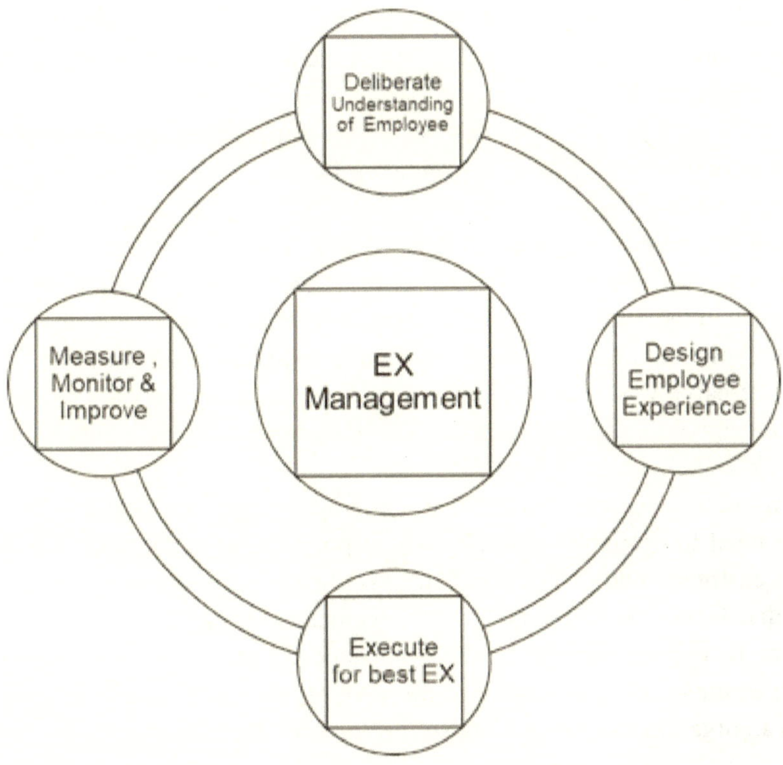

Figure 6.3: EX Management

We need to remember that the whole purpose, to begin with, was to enable customer engagement and success through employee experience.

Some data facts support the fact that if organizations work to engage their staff, they can expect positive returns in their overall business. Here are some of the data points that should encourage you as an organization to continue your efforts on the subject.

- Companies with a highly engaged workforce outperform their competitors by 147% in earnings per share
- Businesses with highly engaged employees show a 19% increase in earnings per share compared to a 3% decrease for those with least engaged employees
- Engaged and motivated employees are 21% more productive than disengaged employees
- Organizations with higher employee experience show better fund utilization in creating rewarding experiences for employees than cost per employee lost
- Companies with the right EX strategies outperform their peers in customer loyalty by 17% and revenue by 11%

Based on recent research by Qualtrics XM institute to assess how employees feel they are treated within organizations across 16000 employees in 24 countries, some very convincing data points are revealed that imply the importance of focusing efforts on Employee Experience.

The research was conducted on two main parameters:

-My primary employer needs to do a better job of listening to my feedback

-I would work harder if my primary employer treated me better

We need to remember that the whole purpose, to begin with, was to enable customer engagement and success through employee experience. Some data facts support the fact that if organizations

work to engage their staff, they can expect positive returns in their overall business. Here are some of the data points that should encourage you as an organization to continue your efforts on the subject.

- Companies with a highly engaged workforce outperform their competitors by 147% in earnings per share
- Businesses with highly engaged employees show a 19% increase in earnings per share compared to a 3% decrease for those with least engaged employees

- Engaged and motivated employees are 21% more productive than disengaged employees
- Organizations with higher employee experience show better fund utilization in creating rewarding experiences for employees than cost per employee lost
- Companies with the right EX strategies outperform their peers in customer loyalty by 17% and revenue by 11%

Based on recent research by Qualtrics XM institute to assess how employees feel they are treated within organizations across 16000 employees in 24 countries, some very convincing data points are revealed that imply the importance of focusing efforts on Employee Experience.

The research was conducted on two main parameters:

- My primary employer needs to do a better job of listening to my feedback
- I would work harder if my primary employer treated me better

Across 24 countries, on average more than 60% of employees agree with both the questions. India tops the list where more than 80% of the surveyed population agree with both the questions, while the Netherlands takes the bottom place with approximately 40% of the respondents to the questions asked. We are not getting in-depth on "why" the responses had been this. The idea is that multiple pieces of research are in place to understand employee disengagement factors. It aligns with future trends of changing work scenarios, so futuristic leaders' expectations have shifted dramatically. The Human Resource functions of companies are undergoing digital transformations that involve technology intervention in the learning and development, and hiring process. The leader's ability to inspire their workforce or trust-building are key factors in their assessment.

It is imperative that Employee Experience will need a much larger perspective and a lot more work than in past and cannot be ignored or neglected at any cost.

EX Management Approach

Basis strategy and simplified approach are explained above, the picture ahead is a representation of how an organization can approach Employee Experience Management.

Accordingly, employee journey maps are key in designing and aligning the employee goals with the company's overall goals. Thus creating initiatives and programs that support experience management.

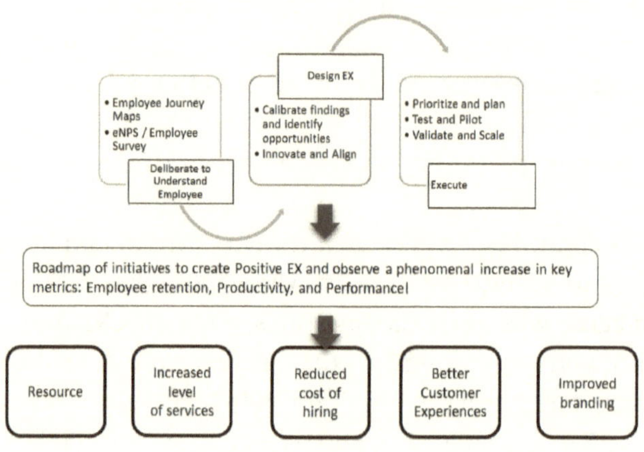

Figure 6.4: Strategy for approaching Employee Experience Management

For deliberating to understand employee behavior, CX offers many tools and techniques that help in accomplishing an insight into the concerns of the workforce. From these gaps or opportunities, organizations could work to build and design strategies to further improve engagement and keep employees motivated.

Along with Voice of the employee, surveys, and in-person interviews, one of the emerging CX techniques that can help achieve this objective is Employee Journey Maps.

A very basic employee journey map is depicted in the picture below:

Stages	Candidacy	Onboarding	Performance	Growth		Exit	Post Exit
Objectives	Find a Job	Understand organization role and goals	Achieve goals, contribute, and receive recognition	Learn, grow and achieve personal satisfaction		Depart organization	Refer and/or return to organization
Employee Experience	Submit resume	Meet and Greet	Management	Learning	Coaching	Exit Strategy	Refer
	Offer Rejection	Benefits review	Recognition	Development	Internal opportunities	Termination	Return
	Interviews	Objective and Role Review	Co-worker relationships	Succession Planning		Resignation	

Figure 6.5: Employee Experience Journey Map

There is a whole method and technique to build these journey maps. And building and drawing Employee journey maps require a few steps:

- A small team of representations from across all functions/departments
- Identify various personas that need focus and attention to build sustainable maps
- Identify the journey of all these personas, basis theirvarious interaction points
- For each interaction point, in a given persona, agreement on specific emotional triggers, behaviors, expectations, or needs of employees.
- Against the needs and expectations also map what is a current provision from the company in terms of policies, processes, systems, or treatment.
- The resulting gaps would be opportunities to improve the experience.
- Validate the gaps with any feedback, interviews, or any other mode of the voice of the employee

It is important that the maps are reviewed and updated at regular intervals and all resulting actions must be run and tested through the pilot first for better assessment.

With the right level of commitment and consistent efforts in building and designing employee experience initiatives, organizations can expect positive results in key employee metrics like attrition, product, and brand performance.

Employees feel valued and motivated to deliver their work as they understand the impact and correlation to organizational goals. The effect of positivity in employee sentiment is exhibited across company culture and evident also in customer interactions. There is improvement in customer service levels as employees feel empowered to make decisions and reflect empathy in interactions with clients. Employee loyalty and focus on their growth and development not only reflects good brand value but also manages operational costs and cuts down costs on new employee hiring or training for these new resources.

The organization needs to treat its employees the same way it expects them to treat customers. The leaders need to balance their focus and attention across all stakeholders, be it, employees or customers, or any other.

As stated above, employee expectations are shifting drastically.

The 'Great Resignation' demands an effort to work through setting eyes on the 'Bigger Retention' approach. The term, great resignation, was coined by Professor Anthony Kotz, recently. A recent article by Forbes suggests that there is a fundamental change in employee expectations and is here to stay.

As the global workforce trends are shifting to dissolved global boundaries, hybrid work culture, and a unique mix of various generations being managed together, leaderships have challenges on their plate to ensure the smooth running of the business.Future leaders are expected to be resilient, empathetic, innovative, and visionary.

For ease of understanding and learning here is a success story of a leading brand in America that managed a complete turnaround in their business results and brand value with employee sensitivity.

Employee Experience Success Story of Campbell Soup Introduction

Campbell Soup Company, which goes by the brand Campbell's is one of the leading processed food and snack companies in the

U.S.A. Their flagship product, Canned soups, is popular with American consumers and stands out in the market with its classic red and white tin packaging.

They expanded their horizons in processed foods, canned meals, beverages, and snacks and claimed the top position in the industry. The company started in 1869, with a history of more than 150years.Today it stands strong with about 14,000 employees across North America and about 8.5 million dollars' worth of net sales in 2021. The brand takes a lot of pride in finding a place in the kitchen of 95% of American households.

The backstory of Campbell's Employee Experience Initiative

Like any other company with a history of more than a century, Campbell's also went through its share of ups and downs in the market, leadership changes, mergers, etc.

In the later part of the 1990s, the brand suffered stiff competition from the market. Condensed soup, the best-selling product, suffered a drop in sales. In 2001 Douglas Conant, the new CEO, had a huge responsibility of saving the company from losses and surviving the threat of being taken over by other industry giants.

It was commendable how he changed the script of the Campbell soup company from total failure to complete success in not more than 8years. Many strategies like cost-cutting, technology interventions, innovations, and marketing made this transformation possible. One specific strategy that played out for him was his obsession with keeping employee engagement in the front and center.

In one of his interviews, Conant stated, "To win in a marketplace, we believe you must first win the workplace".

Starting on Employee Experience Journey

In one of the interviews conducted by Forbes, Conant shared some interesting insights about his beginning on improving employee engagement.

His concerted efforts toward his employees started with committing to his workforce even before demanding any loyalty in exchange. He made an unremarkable start by putting out a Campbell Promise that read, "Campbell valuing people, people valuing Campbell." The organization would stand by its promise in all situations. He also made sure this promise was not just some wise words written but used in any given opportunity to reflect it in actions and decisions.

During one of his visits to a facility in Camden, New Jersey, he noticed how barbed wires surrounded the whole fencing. The place felt more like a minimum-security prison than a corporate headquarters. Removing wires helped build trust in the workforce and gave them a sense of value and respect.

Another impactful action was that over three years 350 existing leaders were replaced by 350 new ones, of which more than half, were filled organically. It helped send a strong message of hope and recognition across the board.

When ideas aren't tied to organization policies and existing systems, they lose their edge. A few of the policy changes decided were:

- A once-in-a-year employee survey was introduced and conducted at the same time for all employees.
- Performance Management review with the direct reports focusing on the goals
- The Manager evaluation included their ability to inspire trust
- Celebrating success and recognizing performers
- Regular personal connections of leaders with employees

As of date, the employee is an integral attribute of Campbell's purpose, vision, and four strategic pillars. Employee experience was the center of all decisions. Campbell's holds a top position in the industry because of its continued emphasis on employee engagement and culture.

Results achieved by Campbell's

It took disruptive ideologies from Conant and some dramatic changes to achieve an outstanding result report over seven to eight years. The company completely turned around its results to par extraordinaire on all fronts. To state a few:

Gallup, a leading research firm, reported remarkable improvement in employee engagement numbers. The results showed:

- 68% of all employees engaged vs. 62% of all employees not engaged in 2002)
- 3% of employees actively disengaged vs. 12% of actively disengaged employees in 2002
- Campbell's earnings jumped by up to 4% over eight years.
- The total return on Campbell's stock, assuming reinvested dividends was more than 30% over that period.

Takeaways from Employee Experience in Campbell's

Campbell's success story stands out with employee experience playing a critical role in turning around its growth and success. A few of the learnings from this spectacular case are:

- There is no substitute for leadership commitment when it comes to the foundation of employee experience
- Employee Experience is driven through integrated vision, purpose, policies, and processes.
- The impact of employee experience is not just about some business metrics but instead a cultural shift that is an immense hike in brand value
- Building trust with an open, transparent, and honest environment is a pathway to stellar employee engagement
- Deliver on promises you make to your workforce
- Listen to the employees at every given opportunity and incorporate the feedback
- Focus on employee growth and development
- Recognize people for their contributions and include them in celebrating success
- Leadership hiring to include ways to assess the ability to inspire employees and generate trust
- Employee experience also impacts overall company growth and merits.

Campbell's story can be used as a proven model to understand and establish strong employee experience within an organization to drive business growth.

Key takeaways for decision-makers

- Consider Employee Experience as a program that is integrated well with overall organizational objectives and larger transformation initiatives.
- It has to be treated holistically, considering all dimensions, and designed strategically with clear goals in mind.
- Employee Experience is critical not only for achieving improved employee engagement scores and lower attrition but also impacts an organization's brand value and customer success.
- The employee ecosystem is also undergoing a tremendous change, given global scenarios, diversity, and decision- makers need to be aware of future trends to deliver the desired experience.

Notes

Part 3

Improving Customer Experience Management

CHAPTER SEVEN

MEASURING CUSTOMER EXPERIENCE MANAGEMENT

If you measure, you can improve - Philips Kotler

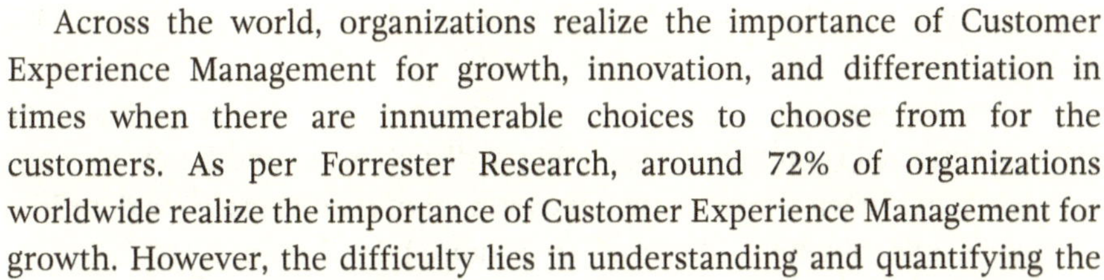

Across the world, organizations realize the importance of Customer Experience Management for growth, innovation, and differentiation in times when there are innumerable choices to choose from for the customers. As per Forrester Research, around 72% of organizations worldwide realize the importance of Customer Experience Management for growth. However, the difficulty lies in understanding and quantifying the customer interactions, thoughts, and emotions to create "Customer Value."

Customers and businesses have come a long way from the era of production and sales with limited offerings and choices to the interconnected world we inhabit today filled with information, opinions, and knowledge. Nevertheless, interconnectedness, information, and knowledge influence customer choices, behaviors, needs, and expectations. As a result, all of it has a significant say in the organization's quality, nature of experience, and deliverables. Customer expectations are rising with knowledge and choices available, and hence Customer retention and loyalty get a lot of focus from organizations to align goals and objectives with it.

Customer Experience Management (CXM) is about **perceptions** drawn by customers at different touchpoints throughout the entire customer life cycle. Customer Experience Management (CXM) is about perceptions drawn by customers at different touchpoints throughout the entire customer life cycle. Customer perception forms a critical criterion in the form of an impression or image in a customer's mind about a company, its offerings, and its products.

Therefore, it affects buyers' choices in selecting or considering a company's products or services. For instance, consider the example of homegrown women's cosmetics unicorn "Nykaa." You will notice that its logo is in "Pink Color," which is usually associated with women. Just looking at the logo creates a perception or an impression in the customer's mind. Or grey, being associated with neutral or luxury brands like Wikipedia or Apple. Perception influences customers' buying, association, and loyalty choices.

Research emphasizes that expectations influence customer perceptions. Expectations in the form of beliefs and knowledge affect perception. Research by MIT shares that expectations or prior beliefs affect our perception in the present, influenced by earlier experiences and thought processes.

Hence, for CXM, carefully designed, implemented tools and processes can positively influence customer behaviors to match or exceed customer expectations, transforming happy customers into loyal customers and ambassadors of products or services.

When we say the term "Customer Experience," the word customer refers to internal (employee; stakeholders; distributors) and External (end-user). It starts when a prospect enters a funnel of awareness, consideration, influence, and buying to become an acquired customer. CXM is across multiple channels via direct (customer service/sales etc.) or indirect connects (website/mobile app/chat).

As per Kaplan, "You can improve what you can measure", thus, measuring across all channels is imperative to an organization intending to be on the path of continual improvement. It requires a thorough understanding of critical KPIs (Key Performance Indicators) for greater "Customer Experience."

Measuring Customer Experience

Measuring Customer Experience Management (CXM) to understand the current state and improve it further involves aligning the people, processes, and products with business objectives for engagement across the complete life cycle of the customer.

Today's digital age and the interconnected world have ensured that customers have more information about different brands, products, and services. Customers share information about their choices and viewpoints, and hence their point of view is essential even while designing the products and services. The "Empowered Customer" era is better informed and has a necessary voice on how businesses and brands work. For instance, even when an entrepreneur or a decision-maker starts working on an idea to create a "problem- solution fit" followed by a "product-market fit," aligning, measuring, and understanding customer problems and expectations are vital first steps. As the business moves forward and grows, those fundamentals start getting implemented at scale. It is fair to expect metrics and measures also advance to assess customer experience on a deeper level. It ensures customer centricity and uses it for driving decision-making and sustainability of the organization.

As seen in the previous chapter, measuring customer experience has to be with the ultimate aim to

- Create POSITIVE EMOTIONS
- Generate TRUST
- Lower CUSTOMER EFFORT
- Enable IN TIME and INFORMED Decisions

Thus it seamlessly involves clarity of purpose with values and consistent organizational actions.

A Customer Experience framework and roadmap, when implemented, will need a host of metrics at critical touch-points. Unfortunately, the metrics and all frameworks can get complex and, at times, lose touch with even organizational goals and purpose (McKinsey report, see details in notes). Measuring CX initiatives sometimes goes even to the level of measuring customer experience itself, which is confusing with broad insights produced that are incoherent and don't support the organizational purpose for a single coherent way to create one way of working.

Thus, four significant steps are outlined to take over this difficulty to measure and improve deliverables through customer experience.

1. Organizational Customer Experience Management (CXM) maturity assessment to quickly assess the current stage.
2. Creating a roadmap of CXM through a framework by aligning customer experience metrics with organizational goals and purposes.
3. Framework assessment also involves creating a roadmapfor engagement by aligning entire stakeholders, including employees, and vendors to know how and what affects CXM. It requires customer journey mapping by integrating people, products, and processes.
4. Metric further (detailed in the next chapter) measures the experience as per the goals achieved across the entire journey or critical touchpoints. The part of the framework is essential to link organizational value and purpose.

Some of the metrics one can derive from measuring and improving customer experience are Customer Loyalty, Customer Acquisition, Customer Effort, and many others. These are used as great markers for businesses' short-term and long-term growth.It ensures that the customers will buy or use existing services and try more products/ services.Furthermore, those products/services shall meet customer needs and expectations and lead to positive word of mouth, emotions, and references.

Further sections talk about the framework and the metric in the next chapter.

First Step: Classifying Organizations Customer Experience Management Maturity Level

An organization can be at a different stage depending on its objective, operations, and above all, its business model. Therefore, the business model and brand positioning become a primary motive for the organization's approach to customer experience management.

A Harvard study demonstrates frictionless journeys and memorable experiences directly correlate with consumers' purchase behavior. However, after a certain point, it becomes zero-sum gains to pursue both together and flawlessly as a strategy. An organization in a mass-market product like Amazon, McDonald's, etc., needs to focus on frictionless journeys more due to the complexity of operations and the scale at which they operate. After a point, it becomes essential for them to maintain their customer connection by delivering on promises. Memorable experiences at some touchpoints will be the perk to enhance retention. However, boutique operations and business models like upscale restaurants and wellness firms need to consider a competitive strategy that focuses on creating memorable experiences that are more personalized and customized to individual preferences (Lucy et al., 2021).

Customer Experience is a sector agnostic concept that is built with customers at the center. However, the maturity in people, processes, and products /services can alter with different organizations and the business model they are pursuing. We cannot ignore the fact that every organization is unique and must come up with a strategy that is relevant to its mission, vision, demographics, culture, people, and customer segment.

With all the differences intact CX provides us with an opportunity to classify organizations based on the level of maturity in their processes, policies, technology, and people they have acquired over some time. This framework is called Customer Experience Maturity Level Assessment and one can find several Cx assessment models based on it.

Further, is an example of the model that we use with our clients. This talks about the various levels we consider to categorize an enterprise. This is backed by different methods and analytical techniques before we conclude on a level for the target company. It is a good starting point and comes with a 30,000 ft assessment of what is in store for an enterprise to be on this journey of Customer Experience Management.

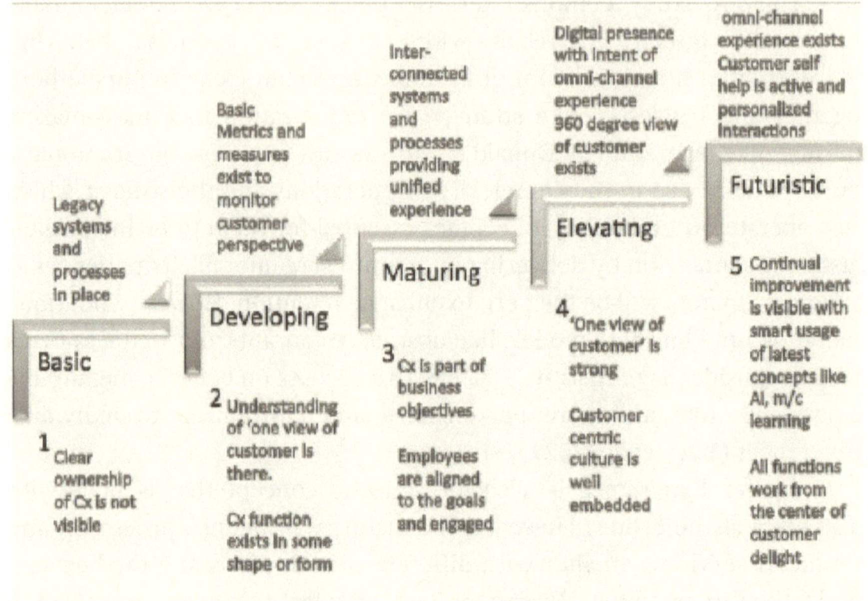

Figure 7.1 – Organizational Maturity Model

Each level in the maturity model is summarized below for better understanding. Once you finish reading this, get an idea of where your organization stands on this maturity ladder.

Level 1: Basic

Legacy channels are there for an organization at a basic level, and "customer experience management" is a shared responsibility. Understanding the "one view" of the customer in an organization is at the primary level.

Clear ownership of CX is not visible at this level.

Level 2: Developing

For an organization at the developing level, traditional channels are there, and "customer experience management" is evolving with the development of the basic "One View of the Customer" at the organizational level.

In addition, there is a dedicated Cx function with some measurement and improvement systems in place.

Level 3: Maturing

For an organization at maturing level, systems and processes are connected. Therefore, there is a unified and consistent technology/process experience across the organization.

CX is a business objective for the internal customers at the policy level with growth and improvement objectives.Therefore, the organization is aligned with the customer experience objectives of engaging internal customers.

Level 4: Elevating

For an organization at an optimizing level, the organization has a digital presence with cross and Omnichannel capabilities for a consistent experience. The internal customers have "One view of the Customer," and the consistent experience has a 360-degree customer view.

Customer insights through measurements, and feedback analysis drive strategies and customer-centric culture across the organization.

Level 5: Futuristic

For an organization at the Futuristic level, Omnichannel capabilities are entirely built for a consistent experience across geographies, places, and products. In addition, customer self-help is enabled with human interference for ease and a "WOW" customer experience.

The Customer Experience Management Maturity level is used not only to find out the current level for the organization but can also be utilized to set a CX roadmap for the future by identifying the target level an enterprise would like to achieve. This framework is a great starting point for organizations who want to take this road of CXM and bring structure and method to the aspirations and goals.As we said maturity assessment is only a starting point, once we know the level , the next step is to figure out our metrics and measure for us to stay objective and identify gaps or opportunities to improve.

This leads us to our second step

Second Step: Framework to Identify Metrics & Measure Customer Experience

Framework for measurement establishes the roadmap and path to improve and brainstorm better solutions for engaging customer experience. The main goal of customer experience is to enhance customer engagement. The framework from the last chapter will support decision-makers on different aspects of the customer experience in their organization. The measures define the broad organizational objectives structured with the customer journey. However, it will need measurement at various levels to know the current "As-is" state and future. It is necessary to measure ROI and demonstrate how different programs perform. Metrics help achieve it.

This framework links the customer journey experience with the holistic business goals. It starts with knowing the customer and aligning the business goals, objectives, products/services, and processes. Then, measurement shall help evaluate the current state and progress needed in customer experience and customer engagement alignment with the business objectives.

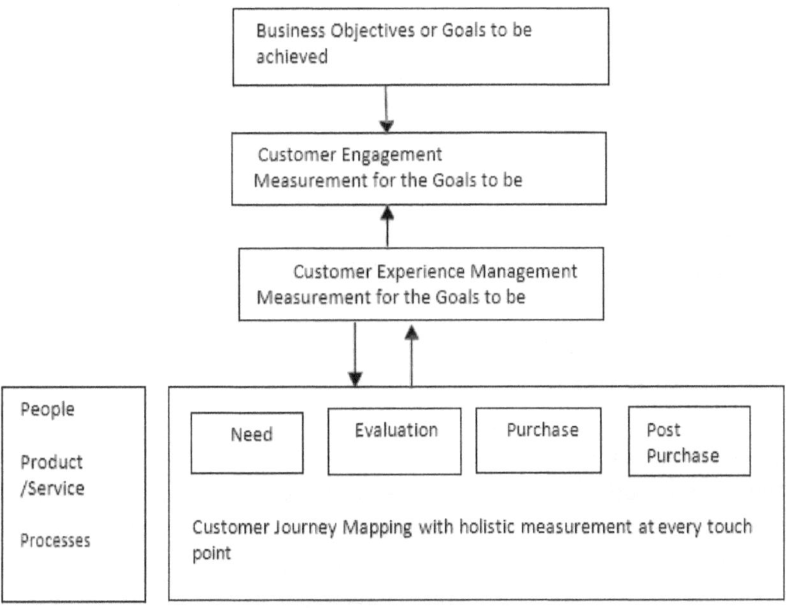

Figure 7.2 – Framework to Measure Customer Experience

The framework consists of four main aspects, namely,

Business Goals and Objectives

Business goals and objectives aligned with the purpose of the organization's existence help to tune outcomes per customer needs and expectations.

Some of the pertinent questions that shall help to align this involve answering -

- What is the customer problem the organization is solving?
- How is the organization making a difference?
- How do business goals and objectives contribute to organizational Vision and Mission?

Business goals and objectives aligned with the organizational vision become the guiding force for employees and vendors. In addition, it ensures initiatives' tactical and strategic actions are aligned to achieve customer outcomes.

Once the business goals and objectives are structured, the next step is to align customer engagement "Current state" and further plans to achieve.

Third Step: Framework Assessment to create a roadmap for engagement with stakeholders

Customer Engagement

Customer Engagement is how the business engages with its customers, affecting sales, brand loyalty, retention, and differentiation (Al Dmour et al., 2019). In addition, customer engagement leads to an emotional connection where engaged customers have more trust, commitment, and positive emotion toward the brand, supporting short-term and long-term growth.

Customer engagement is also about "Knowing the Customer." It is to cater to their needs and requirements by understanding customer behavior, including motivations, attitudes, preferences, and needs, above all the problems which need to be solved. But, most importantly, it is about understanding customer problems to establish a positive emotion and connection.

There is a strong business case as well through research. A study published in a Harvard Business Review titled "The New Science of Customer Emotions" argues that customers who are engaged emotionally with the brand are

- At least three times more likely to recommend an organizational product/service.
- Three times more likely to re-purchase and Less likely to shop around (44% said they rarely or never shop around)
- Emotionally engaged customers are much less price- sensitive (33% said they would need a discount of over 20% before they defect).

Further, the Customer engagement goals and objectives get streamed out from organizational goals and objectives. And also are impacted by customer experience strategy and actions.

Some questions for customer engagement goals involve,

- How are the product and services serving per customer needs and expectations? And most importantly, do we understand customer needs and expectations?
- What is the outcome for the customer through the product and service my organization provides?

So, this essentially means understanding your "Customers" is essential. We further provide you with three tips to "know your Customer."

1. Don't Make Assumptions

The first is Don't Make Assumptions that you know your customer's preferences and beliefs, basis your gut feeling or past practices. If you are starting on a new idea, researching your customers, using traditional surveys, focus groups, and observational/ethnographic studies, always work. It all boils down to listening to your customers. Talking to just a couple of customers can answer crucial questions for insights on a tight budget.

Each day our customers are changing. New technologies, thought processes, and awareness makes customers more empowered and knowledgeable than the product/service providers.

Earlier customers were comfortable with physical merchandise shopping but now they prefer everything delivered to their doorstep with a click of a button, using mobile apps and websites. This is not just true for commodities through e-commerce but also applies to entertainment. Earlier TV and radio were excellent platforms for the content viewing habits of customers compared to current times. Today the customer is more comfortable with 24/7 streaming of content of choice on different platforms such as Netflix, Amazon prime, etc. The web-based entertainment/content-based entertainment business is leaving traditional theaters in dire straits.

2. Empathy

Empathy is an essential tool to understand your customers. Interacting, seeking, and consolidating observations, talks, and discussions from all stakeholders (including employees), on the 'why' and 'how' of needs, expectations, and deliverables can help accomplish a superior customer experience. Insights should also include feedback from social media platforms such as Facebook and Twitter for customers' buying patterns and behaviors or habits. For instance, Zappos global shoes and online merchandise platform, call their Customer Support Staff as Customer Loyalty team. This team listens to their customer's problems and is empowered to suggest solutions naturally without a prior script. The inputs, through opinions and feedback, are further used to improve upon their deliverables. Zappos is a global leader in Customer Experience and has been able to engage with stakeholders in a meaningful way and create a customer-obsessed culture. Nothing beats a human-centric touch to get deeper into customers' pains, needs, and challenges.

3. Customer Journey Mapping Persona

The third important tip is to walk in the Customer's Shoes through Customer Journey Mapping Persona. Customer Journey Mapping (CJM) creates a graphical representation by anticipating customer emotional experiences with an organization for pre-purchase and post-purchase scenarios. CJM supports detailing problems and trust deficit issues for every interaction point in the customer journey. This is an amazing approach to designing positive experiences for all stakeholders, The individual personas can make a clear case on the interactions leading to, for example, attrition or retention, and find solutions for more positive memories and building trust for an enhanced experience. We will talk more precisely about creating "Customer Journey Mapping" in the subsequent sections, and you can do it for yourself in your organization.

Customer Experience Management

Customer Experience Management leads to greater customer engagement. As per the framework in figure7.2, it involves carefully designed processes to engage with customers for a positive perception across the complete journey at all touchpoints. Consistent, predictable customer experience reduces cognitive, physical, and effort in time for organizations while meeting or exceeding demands and expectations.

Customer experience Management needs constant work by defining, measuring, and improving through best practices across the entire journey. Magic of Customer Experience (CX) lies in its wholesomeness and is not an isolated initiative that runs in silos. Organizational interdependencies need integration through policies, people, products, or processes. Hence, aligning the 4Ps with a top- down view will lead to assessing every component for its current state and what it may take to bring it to the desired state.

A top-down view means starting from the objectives and goals of companies to integrating customer experience outcomes for reaching a desired customer engagement state. As a CX-enabled organization, imagine and create a business structure where customer-centricity is the focal point and the entire organization leans towards this centralization.

Customer Journey Mapping with the holistic measurement at every touchpoint

As a business owner or decision-maker, Customer Journey Mapping supports evaluating the experiences of target customer segments and creates a unique differentiation, solutions, and positioning. It is valid for a startup, matured organization, or any business, be it a homerun baking stunt, small-scale online selling, publishing, e-commerce, etc.

The point to note is that every organization also has multiple customer segments and journeys. In addition, an interconnected world and information availability have enhanced the complexity of customer journeys. Customer Journey Map (CJM) as a tool visualizes customer interactions with a brand/organization across all touchpoints. It's a visual story of the interaction, perception, and experience of a prospective buyer persona or a customer of the offering at all relevant stages of their journey, from the first stage of identifying with the need for the product/service to the next phase of evaluating it, followed by a purchase, and post-purchase stage.

A 360-degree view of the customer is built through Customer Journey Mapping. It also involves re-evaluating business strategies from a different perspective, i.e., always keeping the customer in the center of products/ services, processes, and people. The process helps gather valuable insights into the consumer's feelings, motivations, expectations, questions, or concerns at every interaction point through well-researched Personas.

The picture below is an example of a persona depiction for a startup that builds Customer Relationship Management (CRM) products.

And we further outline the process of how you can create your own "Customer Journey Maps" for different personas.

	Persona Details (Bio)	Scope of CJM	Motivation to choose this persona
	A person in mid20s. Belongs to hospitality industry. Is proficient in using all channels. Very high on customer emotions Runs hotel in south India and is keen to grow. Open to invest.	To understand the customer behavior throughout the entire life cycle	The product is mainly focused on hospitality industry and current customers belong t this segment

Figure 7.3: CRM Technology for Restaurants – Persona Overview

Customer Journey Mapping is a holistic, visual, and tangible tool to understand customer needs, expectations, and emotions at each phase of the customer life cycle. Customer journeys are getting increasingly complex, and hence mapping helps evaluate experience, emotions, and deliverables in one frame. The CJM map can be built with a four-step process. The process involves identifying relevant personas followed by creating a common platform with representation from all departments/ functions and all stakeholders to brainstorm experiences of desired personas throughout the lifecycle, identify opportunities to improve, and recommend solutions.

1. Create a Buyer persona

Persona is the personality, attitude, emotions, and motivation of different fictitious people for representation purposes. Different persona is created after understanding customer goals, motivations, and needs at different product or service touchpoints.

How can you create the buyer persona –

- Understand through research about target buyers of your product/ service. Target customer interviews, feedback, social media analytics, and many tools that can support it.
- Create as many personas as you can. A varied persona concerning gender diversity, income /demography/educational changes, or attitudinal references is a good way to start.
- Map these fictitious personas' motivations, goals, and problems for which they need support, or you are providing solutions to these problems.

2. Visualize and Map end to end journey of the customers when interacting with your brand

Visualize, Understand and Map your **Customer's journey and engagement** with your organization throughout the entire customer lifecycle. The end-to-end lifecycle is depicted through touchpoints when the Customer interacts with the organization. It can be offline or online.

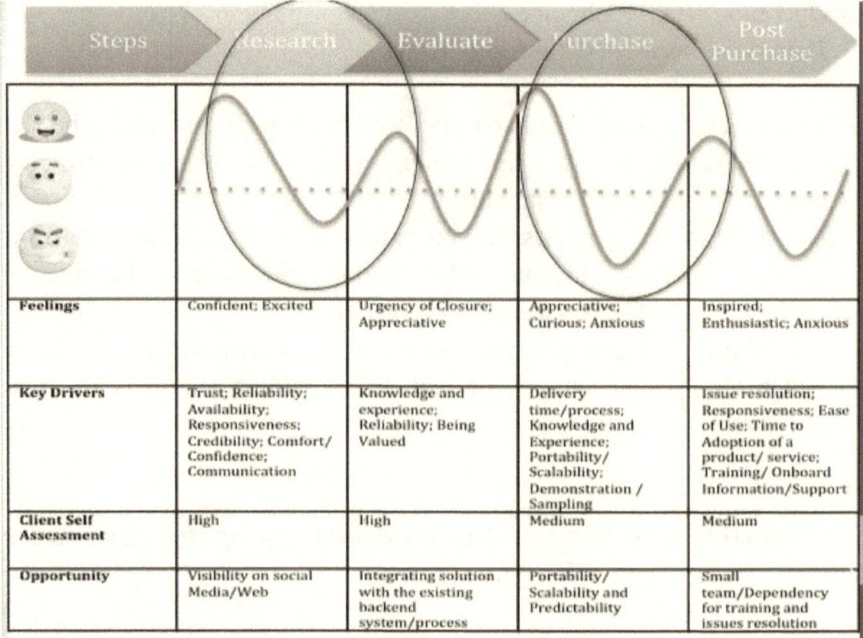

	Research	Evaluate	Purchase	Post Purchase
Feelings	Confident; Excited	Urgency of Closure; Appreciative	Appreciative; Curious; Anxious	Inspired; Enthusiastic; Anxious
Key Drivers	Trust; Reliability; Availability; Responsiveness; Credibility; Comfort/ Confidence; Communication	Knowledge and experience; Reliability; Being Valued	Delivery time/process; Knowledge and Experience; Portability/ Scalability; Demonstration / Sampling	Issue resolution; Responsiveness; Ease of Use; Time to Adoption of a product/ service; Training/ Onboard Information/Support
Client Self Assessment	High	High	Medium	Medium
Opportunity	Visibility on social Media/Web	Integrating solution with the existing backend system/process	Portability/ Scalability and Predictability	Small team/Dependency for training and issues resolution

Figure 7.4: Customer Journey Map created for a restaurant

Customer Journey Map plots the path customers take in interacting with your organization – from the earliest stage of product awareness to purchasing decisions, including onboarding, usage, support, and renewal.

Thus, it includes four stages primarily.

- Need - When the Customer is considering or has the "Need" of a product or service. And this stage of advertisement, word of mouth, PR, website, and google ranking make the customer move to the next step.
- Evaluation - At this stage customer starts evaluating various offerings, substitutes, and complementary products/services. Direct mail, product app, agent connect, and a website can make a difference at this stage.
- Purchase - when the Customer comes to this stage, they avail, buy or subscribe to a product/service.
- Post-Purchase – Reliable post-purchase support, the renewal strategy, and engagement through regular communication can motivate customers to renew their contract, repeat their order or buy a different item or even recommend the product/service to their peers.

Also, it needs to be noted that some touchpoints are more critical than other touchpoints. For instance, onboarding a customer can lead to severe retention and customer loss issues if not handled properly.

Medium: There are many digital solutions available today to assist in creating journey maps, however, start the effort with a rough sketch on board using other aids like paper, markers, or sticky notepads. Once the journey map is detailed and the process is understood, investing in a solution that helps make journey maps portable, accessible and reusable is a great step. Note that journey maps are not a one-time exercise but one needs to keep updating or revisiting them for any changes or progress.

3. Behaviors when the Customer is moving from one stage to another stage

Behaviors, interactions, and organizational deliverables mapping can identify opportunities to improve customer experience. However, it also involves the moments of truth that **make orbreak your engagement with your customer.**

- Understand Customer Behavior including expectations, motivations, and what they are looking for when interacting with a brand/organization across touchpoints. Prior qualitative research for different personas, feedback reports, website analytics, sales-report, and employees' perspectives comes in handy to support and build this understanding.
- It is contextual and relevant for the customers. For instance, a touchpoint that is important and affects customer retention is still not prioritized. Post-purchase engagement with a customer can get a miss in the pursuit to attract more customers.
- Reduces the Customer's mental/physical/time-based effort by understanding and simplifying the easy and efficient journey for the Customer. Data and feedback will help evaluate each touchpoint that needs prioritization to create the required experience.

When mapping customers' interaction with the organizational touchpoints, it is a good idea to identify the key "Moments of Truth." "Moments of Truth" represents a point where a critical event happens. An opinion gets formed about the organization and its deliverables at this juncture. Therefore, it's essential to identify the "Moments of Truth" for innovative solutions and experiences.

It is also classified as Zero Moment of Truth (when online information about a product is searched), First Moment of Truth (when the customer sees the product for the first time), Ultimate Moment of Truth (touchpoint where significant opinion about the brand is formed)

Action plan for implementation

Journey maps support understanding the gaps, like operational inefficiencies caused by multiple or unnecessary handoffs. The Action plans built from such moments of truth help prioritize solutions, allocate and deploy resources and stay focused to provide optimal value.

When adopted correctly by practitioners, it's a discipline that enables employees to shift their perspective from their own to more Customer's views. Specifically, journey maps created through extensive discussions with key relevant stakeholders can minimize individual bias and create a holistic view. It is insightful and tremendously engaging for the employees.

Eventually, a standard and common understanding of customer expectations across the organization and an Omni-channel presence would lead to a frictionless journey and streamlined communication.

When implemented correctly, Customer Journey Mapping (CJM) helps drive customer loyalty, reduces operational and related costs to brand positioning, and maintains consistent messaging across all channels that a consumer would adopt to interact with a product or service.

Advantages of CJM

- Cross-team collaboration and awareness of Customer Experience.
- Strengthen customer focus and **create empathy** for your customers.
- Accelerating **innovation** as identification of make or breakpoints helps create a "Wow" experience.

When combined with metrics at critical touchpoints, this framework can be used to measure and improve.

In the next chapter, we detail the various metrics that can be deployed. We also work on how all metrics need not be used. It depends on the goal to achieve so that metrics can support it.

Meanwhile, a case study to simplify your understanding of customer journey mapping for you.

Case

Breaking Silos for enhanced Collaboration using Customer Journey Mapping as a tool

It is the case of a legacy organization that provides learning solutions in digital and print across the major economies for varied customer segments, including professionals, fresh graduates, students, etc.

The organization has had dedicated print solutions catering to a wide range of customer segments for decades. However, it also started providing digital learning solutions with the advent of time.

The key strength of the organization has been dedicated teams, products, solutions, and continuous research work to add value to its customers through digital and print learning solutions.

Challenges

Increased competition and digitization needed newer customer experience strategies to engage with customers for greater agility and thus intimacy, specifically for digital products. As a result, customer retention was the fundamental problem area for this product line.

Approach

It was essential to derive a customer perspective integrated with sales, marketing, and product development strategies.

A mechanism was needed to identify customer segments and current product strategy tools.

- The roundtables and interviews with stakeholders helped get an initial understanding. The organization matured in the product development stage and had some informal mechanisms to understand user responses.

- The various teams were occupied meeting their deliverables and dedicated to their own goals. The gap was in aligning them to the overall organizational objective and collaboratively deciding future strategies.

A group that was a mix of critical decision-makers and doers from all departments was identified. It was a pilot group to champion this program as a team.

A workshop model was finalized to evaluate and reflect on the gaps since the team was fairly new to customer experience and tools and techniques.

Customer Journey Mapping as a tool was used to draw the appropriate customer expectations gap.

Recommendations & Outcomes

Customer Journey Mapping is a vital tool to comprehend the present state of customer experience at an organization and also put across the evolving behavior and needs basis the expectations. In addition, it supports identifying the opportunity areas for concrete actions to drive discussions and thus align strategies with the organizational vision.

Insights for different customer segments/personas' journeys along the various touchpoints in the organization were gathered.

> *"It supported creating a comprehensive strategy to manage customer experience and present a road map with specific outcomes in line with the organizational vision."*

Following it, the organization built a 360-degree view of consumer insight and created customer service recovery solutions and mechanisms for feedback and insight sharing across the organization, breaking the silos.

This helped them create a roadmap to build more avenues while simplifying the existing consumer processes to engage.

Customer Journey Mapping (CJM) is an incredible tool for differentiating through customer experience in the marketplace. Apart from traditional surveys, customer journey maps canenhance engagement, bring innovative approaches to ease customer effort and thus enhance customer advocacy and loyalty.

Key takeaways for decision-makers

- Customer expectations with prior beliefs, past experiences, and thought processes affect customer perceptions. Customer perceptions thus influence customer behavior regarding the purchase, loyalty, and advocacy with a company and its offerings. Hence expectations have to be managed through experience.
- Measurement of customer experience management support in aligning the business goals, objectives, products/services, and processes.
- Customer experience measurement will support the evaluation of the current state and progress needed in customer experience and customer engagement initiatives.
- Customer Journey Mapping is a holistic measurement of experience across the complete customer journey with products, processes, and people aligned with organizational goals and objectives.

Notes

CHAPTER EIGHT

METRICS TO MEASURE CUSTOMER EXPERIENCE MANAGEMENT

Metrics are for doing, not for staring. Never measure just because you can. Measure to learn, Measure to fix – Stjinn Debrouwere

Metrics are an essential part of customer experience, as they help give numbers to vague interactions, behaviors, and deliverables. Metrics can make the difference between your success and failure. It is primarily because CX initiatives work broadly across a company, they will need alignment across various managerial and hierarchical levels driving the culture, values, and priorities. Moreso, the initiatives may take some time, and measuring them and aligning them with the business results can quantify them.

As per Sampson

""*When CX initiatives don't deliver, CEOs cease to support them, plain and simple. Since CX practitioners fully recognize that 'connecting CX with business results is the key to gaining buy-in from*

CEOs, then why does this disconnect prevail?" **"**

Customer Experience can be righteously driven by Customer journey mapping if done correctly. It helps evaluate the customer's perception throughout its journey with the company. The challenge is that most journeys are complex, with multiple touchpoints, varied channels, and objectives.

- A lot of data can be collected, but will it be useful?
- Should the focus be only on quantitative analysis?
- What type of qualitative data is useful?
- What are the critical touchpoints?
- What measures align with our business results?

Customer Journey Mapping (CJM) is essential to reduce the gap of understanding between the customer and the company. Metrics can give some words and numbers to this measurement to gauge deliverables' (product or service) performance and health.

Metrics integrated with Customer Journey Mapping (CJM)

Research and practitioners suggest that measuring the overall journey better predicts customer satisfaction and engagement than measuring satisfaction at individual touchpoints.

McKinsey's research directly points out, that a company's performance on journeys is 35 percent more predictive of customer satisfaction and 32 percent more predictive of customer churn than performance on individual touchpoints (Source: https://uxmag.com/ and McKinscy)

So why bother about individual touchpoints when the overall journey can be measured and evaluated? Yes, overall journey measurement supports indicating how the overall product or service is performing. However, the journey is the culmination of individual touchpoints. So, it means specific touchpoints can make or break customer engagement and experience perception.

Interestingly, a rule provides clarity to this conflict and can be used more widely in industries/companies worldwide. It is called the Peak-End rule. The Peak-End rule is a behavior economics principle that can make a difference in "Customer Experience." As per this rule, customers remember the peak of the experience that could be best (or worst) with a brand along with the journey's end.

For instance, you went to an amusement park with a family. There you had a series of experiences like a ride that kids will be wanting to do again, standing in a long queue, or everyone gushing about the experience while leaving the park.

A few weeks later, this complete trip stays in your mind as a collective experience from all individual instances. In your mind, what may come to you could be when your family or kids were asking and shouting for another ride. Or it could be when all of your family was scared of a ride. And in the end, when probably all of your family was tired, little gestures of kindness from the staff were making a difference.

The Peak and End rule can make a difference in customer experience. As a decision-maker, measuring those "Peak Points", that could be the best or worst experiences, will align with customer engagement goals. Thus, measuring with relevant metrics at touchpoints will aid with data and insights that can make a difference.

Identify touchpoints that make or break your "Customer Experience"

Consider two scenarios to a problem. First, you bought a product from a company that was not up to the mark or was broken. You got angry and reached out to the company representative for the same.

Scenario-1: It took around 3 mins to connect to the company representative. Who listened and, without question, replaced the product.

Scenario-2: It took around 8 mins to connect to the company rep. The representative listened and, without question, replaced the product. The representative also apologized for the problem and inconvenience to the customer. He assured through his communication that the company would look into and ensure that such incidents do not happen in the future.

The representative also thanked the customer for making the purchase and considering the company. Needless to say, customers will remember the experience from Scenario 2. And thus, measuring the satisfaction at this touchpoint to improve the deliverables will make a difference to the customer engagement and loyalty (customer comes back or refers to other people) metrics.

So the ideal way has to be that identify your crucial touchpoints where the customer experiences very high or low emotions across the customer journey. Certain touchpoints can also be created by design, like simplifying the process at the touchpoint, communicating with empathy, empowering the employees for decision-making to enhance customer ease at the touchpoint, or communicating the deliverables and connecting to understand the expectations. It varies from company to company, depending on the product or services they are selling, value addition to customers, and the business goals to be achieved.

Design your Metrics

Numerous metrics can be put for the overall journey or specific functions like digital engagement, customer service, etc. However, you can also deploy metrics to further assist your goals in evaluating customers' behavior and your deliverables.

Every touchpoint or overall journey can be taken as a box wherein specific inputs like needs, problems, challenges, or actions get converted to customer value or solution output. In between this conversion, particular activities by the customers happen.

A decision-maker can evaluate the behavior by putting some number to the behavior by answering questions such as

1. What are the touchpoints that offer a peak experience to my customers?
2. At these peak experience touchpoints, how long are my customers staying?
3. What is attrition at this touchpoint? Do my customers leave my product or service at this touchpoint? or do they continue the journey?
4. What is my customer behavior at this touchpoint? Should I use or create a rule of thumb or heuristics to compare future interactions?

Your peak touchpoints may also need a qualitative study to answer "Why" it happens simply. Qualitative studies measure the characteristics like behavior perceptions and follow the subjective process to inquiry then the objective ones.

We are also defining some metrics below for measurement and improvement at different stages. For our reader's ease, we have divided the metrics into two categories - Standard metrics and specific touch point metrics. These metrics help in quantifying the entire experience.

For instance, the business goals can include revenue share, profits, or market growth. And is supported by

Sales Metrics - on sales in a specific, measurable unit

Loyalty Metrics - quantifiable measure to calculate customers that chose to stay with the company

Customer service Metrics - to measure the effectiveness of customer service through online or phone support

Cost to acquire customers – Cost needs to be managed effectively and optimized repeatedly

Standard metrics like Customer lifetime value measure the value generated. Sales and loyalty metrics form the basis for calculating the overall value after individual touch point measurement. Other standard metrics like NPS (Net Promoter Score), CSAT (Customer Satisfaction Score), etc., provide comprehensive experience quantification or simply the output of various CX measures undertaken in the company.

Standard Metrics to measure your experience or the Outcome Metrics denoting the effect of efforts in CXM

Customer Lifetime Value

It is a metric that helps the company evaluate how much value a business can get out of a customer in an infinite period. Thus, it helps to assess investments in marketing, acquisition, and customer experience and, therefore, supports settling the priorities.

The formula to calculate it is,

*"" Average Annual Customer Profit * Average duration of customer retention ""*

The metric can help the organization devise strategies to ensure that regular purchasers are given some more preference and customers who are having lower lifetime value could be engaged more. It helps to optimize the investment in customer acquisition and retention strategies.

Rather, CLV can be calculated for individual customers as well, through lifetime value. The formula for it is

*""Average Annual Customer Profit * Average duration of customer retention""*

Further, Kellett (2020) defines how lifetime value as four major KPIs for measurement namely, Average Order Value (AOV), Purchase Frequency (F), Gross Margin (GM), and, Churn Rate (CR). They can be calculated as follows,

"AOV = Total Sales Revenue / Total Number of Orders"

"F = Total Number of Orders / Total Number of Unique"

"GM = Total Sales Revenue – Cost of Goods Sold (COGS) / Total Sales Revenue (express the result as a percentage)"

"Customer Churn Rate = (Customers at start of time interval – Customers at end of time interval)/ Customers at start of time interval"

Blanco
When to use

Can be used for B2B and B2C customers both to understand how much the business is spending to acquire and retain customers.

Customer Churn Rate /Customer Retention Rate.

Customer Churn rate measures how many customers dropped out of the business or didn't renew the product/service subscription over a measurable time frame.

""Customer Churn Rate = (Customers at start of time interval – Customers at end of time interval)/ Customers at start of time interval""

Opposite to this is the Customer Retention Rate which measures how many customers renewed the product/service subscription over a measurable time frame.

When to use

Measuring it gives a good idea in the post-purchase customer journey mapping stage for B2C organizations particularly for subscription-based services or in mass-market modelcompanies deep dive into customer behaviors and purchase journey.

Net Promoter Score

NPS is a measure to find the percentage of customers who would recommend a brand or a product/service to their peers or friends. It scores from -100 to +100. NPS categorizes the customers into three categories. The Promoters are people who give the rating of 9 and 10 on a 10-point scale and thus are loyal and satisfied. On a 10-point scale, customers rating from 8 and 7 are passive and satisfied but unenthusiastic. Finally, from 6 to anything below are detractors who are unhappy and not excited about the brand.

NPS is usually about two questions.

First, one is "How likely are you to recommend this company to a friend or colleague?" on a scale of 1 to 10. The second one is simple to understand why so. So the company can either improve or keep continuing the good stuff

When to use

This can be a quick pulse check at any product/service transaction or the overall organization level.

Customer Satisfaction Score (CSAT)

Customer Satisfaction Scores are usually done with annual or periodic surveys to rate customers' satisfaction with a product/service. The measurement scale can be on a Likert or a 10- point scale. CSAT measures the average satisfaction of customers. It usually has some more questions to deep dive into customers' perception of a product/service, quality, expectations from the brand/service, and how the organization deals with the complaints or problems.

Same way even Employee Satisfaction, Stakeholder Satisfaction can be measured to deep dive and understand the engagement levels, motivations, and expectations.

When to use

Periodic or annual surveys to understand how satisfied the customers are with the various deliverables from the organization.

Customer Effort Score

Customer Effort Score on a Likert or 5-point scale tries to understand by rating how much effort customers had to make while going through a journey or buying a product/service. It helps organizations to create a seamless and frictionless experience

The score is usually from 0-to 100.

> *"CES = Customers who gave score of 4 or 5 / Total Number of Responses"*

For example, if 50 customers out of 100 gave you a rating of 4 or 5, your CES would be 50

When to use

At specific touchpoints where digital engagement is there, and in customer service.

Reflection

To get actionable insights from metrics, you must constantly separate noise from data, particularly for quantitative data collected from surveys. Noise is the statistical variation in data and does not depict the real thing.

For example, you might find that the data shows some variations in some months with NPS data. For some months, it is good and takes a downturn for a couple of months. However, when you start deep diving to find particular reasons for the same, you will find that variation in the data had been due to random chance. This is because the NPS represents the entire population, but say only 10% of customers may respond in a particular month. That 10% of customers were unhappy and thus may not represent the whole population accurately. The margin of Error will support this scenario where the NPS can sometimes go up and down around the average mean.

Specific touchpoint Metrics

Plutchik's Wheel of Emotions for Emotional attachment

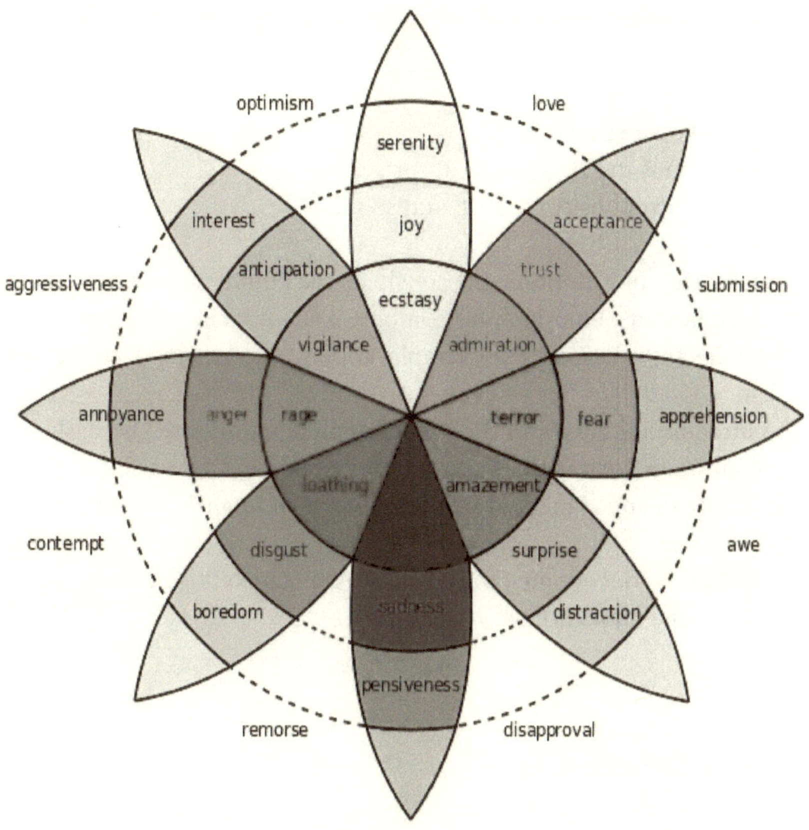

Source: interaction design.org (see notes for more details) Copyright terms and licence: Public Domain

Developed by Robert Plutchik this wheel of emotions helps to define and assess the emotions of internal and external customers at different touchpoints. Understanding emotions support mapping customer behavior, including need and expectations assessment. AI and ML capabilities can be utilized further to enhance the experiences by understanding emotions. As per the wheel of emotions, there are eight primary emotions joy, trust, fear, surprise, sadness, anticipation, anger, and disgust. These eight basic emotions are based on the physiological purpose of each.

In the wheel,

Primary Emotions: Depicted on the wheel are anger, anticipation, joy, trust, fear, surprise, sadness, and disgust.

Opposites to Primary Emotions: In the wheel, opposites to every primary emotion are opposites. Like

- Joy is the opposite of sadness
- Fear is the opposite of anger
- Anticipation is the opposite of surprise.
- Disgust is the opposite of trust, and so on.

Combination of Emotions: In the wheel, the emotions with no color are a mix of 2 emotions. Emotions are complex, and understanding can support building relevant solutions. For example, anticipation and joy combine to be optimism.

The intensity of colors in the wheel depicts emotions: The darker the shade of emotion great is the intensity. For example, anger at its least level of intensity is an annoyance. At its highest level of intensity, it is rage.

When to use

At individual touchpoints and even AI/ML capabilities can be used to enhance human connection with the brand

Customer Service Metrics

Average Time Resolution

Average time resolution is a metric used to measure the total time taken to resolve an issue. Usually, if a lot of time is taken, then certain fixtures through training and processes are suggested. On the other hand, the less time is taken to resolve the issue, the more shall be customer's satisfaction.

"Average Resolution Time = Sum of all times to resolution in a timeframe/ Total number of cases solved in that"

First Contact Resolution

It is about how many issues were resolved at the first contact itself. It helps to measure whether the employees are empowered and trained to support the customers.

Faster resolution and, in the first time itself, leads to greater satisfaction.

"First Contact Resolution = Number of resolved incidents closed on first contact/ Total number of incidents"

Visitor Intent.

It is the metric used by digital businesses to understand why the customer came to the website. Was it for purchase or information? How much time did he spend on every section?

It is by simply seeing customer clicks and tracking the options they visited to know more about them.

Task Completion.

It is a simple metric to measure whether the customer was able to accomplish what he came to the website for. Most of the time, it's a simple YES/NO

Sales Level Metrics

- Incremental purchases from existing customers
- Higher retained revenue as a result of reduced churn
- New Sales were driven by word of mouth
- Monthly Recurring Revenue
- Shipment rate or accuracy of shipment
- **Social Listening:** This metric tracks how and what people talk about a company and the deliverables. Good or bad, it provides referrals and opportunities to an organization to improve the deliverables and its relationship with the people.
- Card abandonment rate

So which metrics to use depends on your touchpoints where peak experiences happen. Overall metrics can gauge the complete health of your entire customer journey, whereas measuring particular touchpoints can provide insights for experience and thus engagement.

The metrics can be for engagement purposes, customer-related purposes, or business-related purposes. The idea is when aligned with organizational goals, the data makes a difference in concrete decision-making.

Data analytics in Customer Experience

Data Analysis is getting more prominence in "customer experience" as a multitude of data is created across multiple channels and customer journey touchpoints. Understanding customer preferences and behaviors allow organizations to create superior experiences for their customers.

Investing in data analysis capabilities means relying on AI and machine learning, which goes beyond traditional research-based quantitative and qualitative approaches. For example, survey-based research lacks real-time data points for decision-making.

It is where AI, ML-based strategies for predictive analysis can aid organizations' real-time decision-making for customer behavior preferences insights.

Organizations seek to create CX programs that are holistic, predictive, and aligned with business outcomes. For example, organizations can collect digital data from customer behavior, interactions, and movement across channels, social media to analog, and digital data from IoT devices. Data Analysis comes with a clear mandate that organizations prefer to understand behavior and preferences as customers interact across touchpoints in the customer journey instead of asking customers about their satisfaction, efforts, etc.

It would mean investing in capabilities to collect vast data from emails, chats, and social media interactions across touchpoints for customers' operational and financial behavior preferences. Handling such extensive data can have limitations as all data may not mean something for decision-making.

Thus, it is pivotal to understand what is driving "customer behavior" basis different personalities and these are the critical indicators of enhancing the experience linked with business results.

Investing in capabilities to identify and generate key CX indicators would mean a change in the mindsets of the teams to utilize predictive analytics to identify pain points, opportunities, and more capabilities as linked with the business results. The understanding of customer journeys in detail would mean identifying attributes for improving machine learning models. These can also be compared with an organizational hypothesis (view) to see if more features need identification for the machine learning model or a fresh hypothesis (idea) for data collection and experimentation.

Artificial intelligence can be used to create algorithms to automate personalization processes for greater customer loyalty or satisfaction from the operational and financial data collected. AI and machine learning aid in predictive analysis based on data collected.

The critical point to be noted here is that the data scientist creates machine learning models. The organization and leadership or CX team set the strategy and direction for initiatives and necessary collaboration between stakeholders, based on inferences derived from outputs of these models.

For instance, the self-service functions that reduce customer service agents' digital load would mean understanding the various use cases—and creating models to coach customers to find answers before connecting to a real agent. The use cases mean analyzing data on how and when customers escalated their problems, what had been the essential questions, or what had been the instances when the system stuck, or a customer moved from one channel to another. Increased Omnichannel presence needs real-time decision- making and processes to enhance customer satisfaction, precisely when an organization scales up and builds to serve customers across markets.

In data analysis, customers' privacy and following the best cybersecurity practices are essential. Governments and customers are becoming extremely vigilant of their confidentiality, and customers particularly like to do business and prefer companies they trust with their data. In the future, customer privacy and how companies are using data can become a source of competitive advantage.

Metrics using traditional survey methodologies or advanced predictive analytics using machine learning models, Artificial Intelligence would mean setting the direction for CX initiatives in sync with business results.

Case

Measures and Metrics in a Manufacturing Organization

It's a case of a manufacturing company based in Delhi/NCR with pan- India operations in the healthcare industry. The company has been in operation for many years. Over the years, a deliberate focus on customers supported it to enhance its reach through a focused product portfolio. The result led to an enhanced turnover, and so have the profits with more customer references sale opportunities, including brand positioning for surviving the perfectly competitive market.

For B2B manufacturing organizations, customer experience goes beyond implementing digital strategies for quick and wider reach like in B2C organizations. Valued addition in the product is the heart of customer retention, acquisition, and innovation focus. Measures and metrics play a significant role in supporting transformation and growth by focusing on objectives while constantly reflecting on deliverables and their value addition to the end consumer.

Situation

The organization has a pan-India presence through partners, various alliances, and dealers. The product is intensely competitive, where international companies have a significant presence, and domestic players also have considerable influence. It's a typical scenario of a high-growth market with companies competing on quality and price. Hence customer retention and references were essential to survive and grow.

"Customer Engagement" aligned with the business objectives.

The organization had the business objectives of year-on-year growth across different product verticals while continuously aligning the organizational deliverables for customers. Digital engagement with customers had the following goals.

- Supporting the buyer's journey with information to support decision making
- To build agility to respond to changes in customer requirements quickly.
- Deliverables for customer satisfaction and advocacy.

Insights into Customer Experience

Over time, including while surviving the pandemic, Customer Experience Management in the organization involved,

- Digitization of customer buyer journey, including providing relevant information through the website, social media channels, and catalogs/ product brochures.
- Customer convenience was focused on product utility demonstrations as per customer convenience by utilizing online video options as well.
- Inventory management and various other operation processes too were digitized to improve the quality and efficiency of operations. CRM and ERP implementation enhanced efficiency with less work duplication and siloed work for a more collaborative and structured way of working for clear deliverables across all the departments in the company.
- Enhanced innovation as collaboration and customer engagement, including internal and external, led to product development, refinement, and improvement insights.
- Customer service requirements also became streamlined with lesser complaints due to complete clarity across the customer journey. The company also focused on providing relevant customer information at crucial touchpoints like the transport journey or when the order was dispatched to add to the customer experience.

Metrics

The company started with metrics mostly related to product experience, including quality and customer budget considerations.

- After every transaction, periodic CSAT Surveys and an NPS helped the company realize customer issues in the buyer journey to create convenience through digitization in demonstrations, products, and other information collateral.
- Customer service metrics like First contact resolution and average time resolution enhanced the service function. The other outcome was insights for product development, workforce training, and appropriate

information deliverable at the right time.

Detailed Csat surveys also helped the company firm the product improvement features and other innovations needed to cater to different target segments and support growth.

More so, it helped the company's brand positioning by creating processes to listen to the customer and be available for support at all times.

Conclusion

B2B companies, typically manufacturing companies, also need customer engagement to manage relationships and the company's long-term growth. Creating customer convenience and understanding the whole paradigm of the outcome of the product can support organizations to develop experience through convenience, relationship management, and service deliverables for more customer satisfaction, loyalty, and advocacy.

Focus on outcomes, on how the product made a difference to the end-user will encompass that organizations create a complete solution-focused to create value for the customer through specific product characteristics and experience around it.

Key Takeaways for decision-makers

- Metrics measurement across the customer journey aligns the customer experience to engagement goals and ultimately the business results
- Metrics support maintaining focus and accountability in the organization
- Metrics can be used to assess customer behavior preferences across touchpoints to aid decision making
- Metrics can be used across the entire customer journey, or specific touch-points and even can be designed in alignment with your business objectives
- Predictive data analysis using AI and machine learning can create superior experiences when working at scale, however, care has to be given to data privacy and cyber security issues.

Notes:

Part 4

Making it right through CXM Governance

CHAPTER NINE

CUSTOMER EXPERIENCE MANAGEMENT GOVERNANCE

"However beautiful the strategy, you should occasionally look at the results." —Sir Winston Churchill

Looking at results regularly and knowing what exactly you are looking at is the simplest explanation of what a Governance plan would entail.

The key to any business program's survival and success is undeniably a strong governance program. A governance program is a layout of a structure that specifies primary and secondary goals from the initiative and the means to monitor and measure desired outcomes.

While we get excited about the structure of the governance plan, let us not forget the key to good governance is more about being clear, focused, and responsible.

For it to be impactful and effective, any governance model must have the following components.

- Committed Leadership & Executive Sponsorship
- Dedicated Council that is responsible and accountable

- Ground Rules or Principles that outline the program
- Effective Communication that is transparent and Timely
- Clear goals and KPIs

Now that we understand what governance implies, it will be easier for us to understand CX Strategy and its governance.

Some of the important questions we will address in this section are:

- Why is it important to have a governance plan?
- How to build an effective CX Governance Plan?
- What could hamper the Governance Plan?

Why a CX Governance Plan?

As Customer Experience (CX) professionals, we need to understand the criticality of designing effective governance around our various initiatives.

Forrester's Predicts report of 2022 released recently states the importance of Customer Experience in a given volatile situation. One of the embarking shares by this research is the fact that one in four CX professionals will lose their job to the increasing demand for proving CX initiatives contributing to the top line/bottom line. It is an ask for every CX professional to now start transitioning CX programs from the experimental phase to the real business game.

So how do we come out of this paradox wherein we are constantly balancing between stressful budgetary constraints, market dynamics, leadership expectations, and effective outcomes of CX strategies and projects?

Forrester Predicts suggests it's time to be bold and decisive in our business. Artificial Intelligence, Technology interventions, customer centricity, and sustainability will continue to be driving forces shaping our business growth and trajectory shortly.

Effective and efficient governance of all the initiatives is our answer to managing these emerging concerns. A firm CX portfolio must be supported by a solid CX governance plan.

These are some of the reasons why we should never ignore working on governance:

- It will enable us to keep an eye on the quality of our projects and strategies and keep us on track to deliver good
- It will help us identify and manage conflicting priorities between business operations or transformations involving technology intervention
- It allows us to demarcate resources, be it human or monetary or
- Any other, and brings clarity to all stakeholders about their involvement and smooth running of projects.
- Most importantly it brings with it accountability and ownership from not only the team but also the sponsors or leadership team

We all know "You can't manage what you can't measure" and a Governance plan necessitates this aspect of identifying the specific outcomes and parameters to measure and monitor those.

Given the latest research and studies, CX is central to an organization's growth and has the power to impact multiple layers within an organization. In the current post-pandemic scenario, organizations have been under tremendous pressure financially, irrespective of their size and industry. As a result, leaders have been frantically looking for answers to improve their top line or bottom line.

When CX claims to be a transformation agent, the pressure is also translated into the teams that take on these business excellence programs. So, if you hold a CXO position and relate to this pressure, you must understand the nuances of defining a strong and efficient Governance program for your CX portfolio.

Customer Experience Professionals Association (CXPA), a leading organization in customer experience knowledge databases, suggests

Adoption and Accountability as key to an effective and complete Customer Experience Management Plan. The governance blueprint is a framework that leads to building these factors for an organization undergoing a transformational journey.

For enterprises to live through this challenge and the CX lead to continuing tracking success, specifically about CX ROI, the governance model helps in unveiling the magic timely and objectively.

With transparency involved and reliable information being shared, employees are driven to deliver their best and draw context to their daily work with customer success.The structure and lean processes, eliminating silos, enables quick resolve to issues and looping actions back to the customer with proactive communication and minimizing recurrence results in outcomes that help build customer trust. It is already explained how customer trust feeds into customer loyalty and lifetime value.

Talking about customer loyalty automatically leads to an important point that we must discuss as we are covering Customer Experience Governance and its benefits. As organization leaders prepare for setting a vision and plan for big gains, a big question that is always debatable is

"Should the company focus more on existing customers, spend their resources in engaging and cultivating repeated business, OR should they be diverting their funds more towards sales and marketing and emphasize on acquiring new clients?"

One could argue what is a big contention here, couldn't companies just focus on both? Well, the answers are not as straightforward.

Several types of research have been funded to figure out if customer retention is indeed more cost-effective than customer acquisition or if customer loyalty or lifetime value is a game-changer for businesses

The Metrics and measures section has already covered the key measures and their importance but with a governance plan in place, one could find answers to key questions that could help drive decisions and have breakthroughs in the customer journey.

Specifically for decisions like choosing customer retention over customer acquisition or vice versa here is how a fine blueprint of governing customer experience effort could deliver:

- Cost markers around specific customer traits like existing customers' vs new customers. One could factor in the cost vis-a-vis returns around the two categories and compare for the specific business.
- Trending tally of business drawn from existing customers compared to new customers. What does the distribution look like?

The governance blueprint opens the diaspora of bringing change makers together, discussing the outcomes, and defining their next steps basis the findings, all in context to the common vision of customer experience goals leading to business success.

Specifically closing on what should be companies focusing on, customer retention or customer acquisition, it all depends on the industry, the company vision, the structure, and results. Most importantly what stage of transformation or growth an organization is in?

Build an effective CX Governance Plan

An old-school method would imply that a governance plan is a blueprint limited to putting appropriate customer-centric metrics in order and laying incentives basis performance on the critical measures.

However, this is not enough in the current scenario. While metrics form an integral part, an efficient CX governance program must follow the 5 principles explained earlier.

Following are a few clear steps to an effective Cx governance model that is comprehensive and enables all parts of the organization to work in tandem keeping customer perspective at the core of all actions and decisions.

Step 1: Clear and, well defined CX Portfolio

The biggest threat to CX initiatives has been a weak business case with no clarity of what the program stands for. So even before we want to create a governance plan, it is important we have a portfolio that clearly outlines the following:

- List all the CX projects that are running across the organization
- Identify the business functions and cases where it is expected to impact
- Identify roles and responsibilities with clear ownership and
- Accountabilities assigned for each project
- Identify the budget and resources

Step 2: Setup a CX Governance Council

CX governance council is a committee that is established to review the progress of projects at regular intervals of time. The council must comprise of:

- Executive Sponsor
- Senior Managers (Representing all departments)
- Key Project Players

Believe it or not, finding a sponsor in the executive committee is the most challenging part but is absolutely a 'must have'. Leaders naturally tend to get occupied with traditional business priorities and move the transformation projects away from their sight.We know CX is a game-changer and calls for an organization-wide transformation, both cultural and operational, and hence a leader supporting it from the front is going to make all the difference. Also, having a council allows you to drive seriousness around the program and give it a model for objectivity and direction.

A cross-functional council with representation from each department, irrespective of their direct involvement in the projects allows transparency and participation across the board.

Step 3: Identify Goals and KPIs

Needless to say, for any project to be sustainable, it must have clear goals that are specific, time-bound, and measurable.

We all know how CX influences various aspects that are directly related to customers. Each project or program in your portfolio must lead to specific outcomes that are defining positive experiences for customers. All these parameters must be quantifiable and directly linked to a crucial business growth outcome. Read Ref Chapter: Metrics and Measures of CX.Any interdependencies between the CX projects or/and any other business initiative should be highlighted and references should be made for the report-outs.

Step 4: Build a Supporting Change Management Plan

Any transformation program may lead to small or big changes across the organization, impacting various aspects of day-to-day business. Often, changes call for resistance from the larger organization if the change is not communicated and contextualized well for each function or impacted employee.

To ensure successful implementation of your CX program, have a well-defined change management plan that clearly articulates every change, timelines, impacted parties, and support in line for working through the change. It is equally critical to highlight how the change is beneficial for the organization and linked to an individual's growth or success. The strength of a change management plan lies mainly in an effective communication plan. Ensure that throughout the program, the communications are being rolled out on time, relevant, and transparent at all times.

With the increasing pressure on budgets and the slow running of businesses, it becomes our responsibility as CX transformation agents to be vigilant to the business demands and work to make CX simple, impactful, and yet transformative.

Reflection

A successful program requires diligent execution, a culture of ownership and commitment, and an effective governance plan. Culture can make all the difference and building it in an organization needs involvement, communication, accountability, and above all, "Trust." Trust needs authenticity, transparency, and empathy. Regular feedback also helps to align, collaborate and work.

As you are building your Governance plan- give a check to your culture to create an efficient execution.

Key factors that hamper a CX Governance Plan

The basics of planning always warn us to take into account any risks that we can foresee and plan for contingencies while we are still at the designing stage. CX governance plan is no exception and hence we would like you to keep the following pointers in mind when you are moving forward with your strategies:

When we are all excited about planning the perfect governance, we tend to get theoretical and blindly go by the books and stand at the risk of ignoring our business realities. So, while we are at it, we must not ignore the uniqueness of our organization, its specific vision, and its priorities. So even before we initiate this step, we must spend time and effort to get to the ground reality and stay as authentic as possible.

One of the biggest risks that stand in the way of a stellar CX governance plan is the one that is built in silos. One of the key factors that will take you progressively in your charter is when you align the intended governance plan with the larger organization charter. Ensure that the stakeholders with fair representation from all departments are regularly involved in the overall governance and implementation. The CX governance plan should not be a stand- alone but rather part of the organization's plan. While driving the wagon, make sure you are not alone in it!

An important aspect to keep in mind when you are owning a CX governance plan is not to be afraid of sharing true results. Always maintain transparency and keep a bulls-eye on results and how they are trending. Hiding facts and not communicating the real picture could completely take away the confidence in CX's intentions, especially when we are at the task of proving our credibility in key organizational goals.

Not being clear in communicating our plan and setting expectations with all involved directly or indirectly is one big reason most of the plans fail. To solidify your governance plan, proceed with key communications for different stakeholders, and keep them relevant, timely, and clear. Ensure that all communications are contextualized for the desired audience and that they feel involved and valued.

The most important parameter to consider when you decide on the council is to ensure that representation is capable of decision- making and influences critical aspects of any program, be it budget, staffing, or any other. More than the number of heads on the project it is important to have competent and efficient participation. So, be sure of who is joining the team and it is absolutely fine to demand the resources that serve program needs.

The diagram further helps us understand the CX governance model:

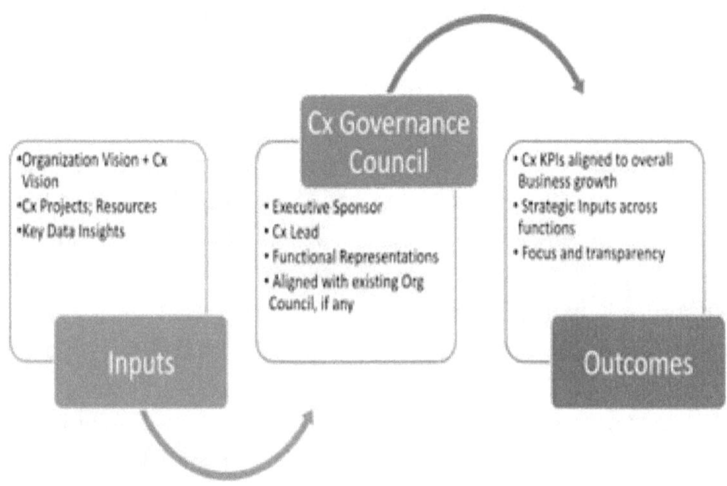

Figure 9.1: CX Governance plan

A case study of an organization that applied CX governance efficiently can help us clarify any questions on how all this ties up together.

Case

Customer Experience Governance Applied in Services Company

Industry: Logistics & Warehousing

Service: Warehousing & on-demand logistics

Deploying a Governance Strategy to Customer Experience Program

Introduction

A well-established mid-size logistic company offers services of warehousing facilities that include rented space, storage, and distribution. They have been in business for more than 5years and cater to several small and medium-sized enterprises across the country.

The biggest challenge that this industry faces is access to timely and accurate information at all times, across various locations, and ensuring a secured stocking facility of goods for their clients at a desired time and place. The provider relies heavily on the demand- supply forecast, goods details, and customer service requests.

This is an industry that is driven by strict service level agreements and works under volatile customer demands requiring the highest scale of stakeholder engagement. The ecosystem itself is very dynamic and time-sensitive which involves several interactions with multiple contacts. With business in multiple cities, the complexities are manyfold with the variety of cultural aspects of the workforce, both blue-collar and white-collar.

The competitive landscape and need for scale-up, left no choice for the organization leaders but to adopt a strong Customer experience program. The charter for an omnichannel experience involved a huge data management exercise, technology intervention, and cultural shift to build customer-centricity.

The Story

Given the nature of this business, complexities were many. The leadership was impressed with the idea of a positive customer experience and agreed to the recommendations of beginning on the path of knowing their customer better and keeping them first in their decision-making.

Within a few weeks, CX COE (center of excellence team) was formed and a CX leader was appointed. Every detail was followed by the books and a clear intent was floated with CX's mission, vision, and goals laid out. The core team and leadership were very excited to begin their journey.

The next step was for this team to build their charter and present the case to the executive committee. The entire portfolio of projects that were to follow from this newly formed setup was to further support and push the following primary goals:

- Dynamic and customized warehousing services to all clients
- Workforce support at the warehouses to provide operational support in packaging, tagging, inventory management, etc.
- Seamless and integrated supply-chain services

The CX charter was well received by the decision-makers and signoff was given on the initiatives. Some of the recommendations from the team that came were:

- Customer Journey Mapping
- Digital transformation to find a more evolved system that integrates CRM and supply-chain, as well as is predictive to forecast demand and supply
- Install structured mechanisms to capture the voice of the customer Now it was time to begin the work!

Something isn't going right!

This was a Monday morning when our office received a frantic call from the CX leader, who happens to be a good friend. He wantedto meet urgently and needed help.

The first sentence that came out of his mouth as we made our way to the discussion room was "Something isn't going right! You got to help me!!"

As a consultant, the key skill we need is "listening" and seeking information to a point where we get to the real problem. So, the conversation started and we knew this one is not going to be short. Without going into the details, we summarized the entire session into two big problems:

1. CX projects were failing deadlines and way behind their target date
2. Leadership team is not available to listen and support

From our experience, we knew where the piercing concern for this leader was coming from. The big underlying stress for him was knowing that he could lose a job for not delivering on the promises he made at the beginning of the program.

We were able to discover the missing dots in the whole design of this structure and charter from the beginning, but there was a due diligence exercise that was required.

We shook hands and signed the mentoring contract with this CX leader to guide him through this challenge. What was commendable about him was that he took a bold step of foreseeing the problem quite early, within 3 months of starting and reaching out to experts for help.

What went wrong?

In so many years of our dealing with businesses, one of the common traits we noticed is that we get excited about new concepts and make an enthusiastic beginning but then we soon start observing un- favoring results. This not only leads to a huge loss in investment monetarily but also demoralizes the team to a great extent.

The reason why things start going south in a lot of cases is that we rush into adopting new concepts and do not spend enough time understanding the details. Some key points we miss are:

- Knowledge of relevance to our current business scenario
- Impact on our current goals and outcomes
- the ask of adoption of this idea in terms of budget, manpower, and time.

This is exactly what went wrong in this particular case that we are discussing. This is where the problem started for them:

Appointment of CX leader

The CX leader in question was appointed from the existing marketing team and was handed over the responsibility with no training and transition time in hand to understand, learn and grow in the role.

- CX team formation

The team members were identified basis availability and not the competence required. There was no great deal of due diligence on the required skills and experience.

- Organization goals not aligned with CX goals

CX's mission and vision were stated inadvertently to meet the key business outcomes. There wasn't enough understanding of how each CX initiative could help achieve specific goals. The CX agenda was set with the ultimate intention of meeting goals but no objective KPIs that would link directly or indirectly to the said outcomes.

Lack of leadership commitment to the program While the executive committee agreed to the idea of implementing CX but no leader was the sponsor for the program or took the responsibility for this effort providing it the support it needed, considering the range of impact it had across the functions.

Recommendations and Steps taken

Resolving all the problems highlighted in the above section was a single-line statement but not that straightforward to make it work.

Recommendation to begin with from us to this leader was: Have a firm CX governance plan in place!

To make this happen, he will have to start with some clean-up exercises and find ways to have some tough conversations with the leaders. The biggest challenge for us in this advisory was to provide him with saving grace in the work he managed in the last three months.

Following are the recommended steps for him to begin with:

- Align and integrate CX charter with other organizational/departmental level programs and highlight interdependencies and suggested impacts.
- Reconvene with the leadership team to share current progress and new findings. It is important to highlight the roadblocks now and share the foreseen risks and way forward. There is no other way!

The way forward in the new charter must include the following:

- A request for an executive sponsor to establish leadership commitment
- Identify CX KPIs and map them to the organizational goals.
- Setup and include CX Governance to monitor and track the portfolio progress
- Assessment of CX-COE team for skills and knowledge required for efficiency in assigned projects. A clear statement of the desired competency with required effort will go a long way in demanding the right resources.
- Prioritize and reallocate some budget to training for self and team in customer experience ensuring that everyone understands basic to expert level of concepts, depending on their involvement and contribution in the project.
- Establish a CX governance council with fair representation from all stakeholders. It must be integrated with any other existing organizational governance body, as applicable.

- Devise a communication plan to share the progress of programs and their impact on an ongoing basis with the core team, executive sponsor, governance council, and larger organization that may include employees and other stakeholders.

There was a lot for this CX leader to accomplish but given his intent to stand by the right he will need just that extra courage to take the first two steps. Once the trust is built with the executive committee and the sign-off given on the proposal, there is no reason why they would not see the benefits of investing in this program.

Results Achieved

Revised CX charter: Approval given after two cycles of rigorous reviews
CX governance council established
With clear monitoring and measuring methods in place, the leadership was always informed of the progress and impact it created. The desired transformation was huge, both operationally and culturally, that would require time but there was an overall trust and acceptance across the board because of timely and transparent communication.

The core team was motivated to work on the projects and even voluntarily agreed to work extra hours. The key organizational goals were tracked with the voice of customers, issue resolution, and customer effort score, all trending upwards.As a result, this warehousing service was able to aggressively work towards its success and create a disruption in the industry with cutting-edge technology and unbeatable customer experience throughout its journey.

Key takeaways for decision-makers

- Governance plan is a must to monitor and track the progress of the customer experience program.
- The findings and review from the governance of the customer experience initiative can be used in building a business case for acceptance of transformation efforts and their results.

- Governance model is a great way to create awareness and impact fully for projects across the organization and build brand value.
- Helps in keeping decision-makers on track with affordability and returns
- Reflects on commitment and sincerity to the program and hence a great way to build trust with customers.

Notes

CHAPTER TEN

EPILOGUE

"Customer Experience isn't an expense. Managing Customer Experience bolsters your brand." —Stan Phelps

Now that we have covered all the basic concepts of Customer experience, it is important to map theories with reality.

Today's world is full of uncertainty and shifting gears at a horrifying speed. It has been a challenge for all of us to cope with these changes, both personally and professionally. CX world also finds itself caught up in the continuously changing ecosystem.

New threats like great resignation, data breaches, digital survival, recession, and others keep bombing the business fraternity and it has become almost impossible to stick to a plan. It seems there is almost no sense in having a plan in the first place! The chaos is also very visible in our ambassadors of Customer experience, who are trying their best to survive the dichotomy of juggling transformation initiatives with the volatilities of the environment and people, be it employees or consumers.

Given the pressure of low customer acquisition and inflation, the focus of our business leaders moves to find ways to generate revenue, reduce operating costs or fight the pricing to beat the competition. As a result, programs like CX initiatives get stalled or deferred infinitely. Even today CX is debated for its returns to the investment and its alignment with larger business interests.

As flag bearers of Customer Experience, we know that given the right amount of time and commitment it shows results in the most amazing ways. Having a strong hold on driving strategies using customer experience management not only helps improve customer loyalty and advocacy or employee engagement but also in long term contributes to collaborated working, and brings in a cultural shift with the feeling of oneness. If done right and well It has the capability of positively impacting every business process that matters.

Keeping customers first in every decision and staying up to date with customer expectations and their buying behaviors is the only way a brand can stay ahead of its competition. Customer Experience Management is the most reliable and effective way of reaching that goal of being the market leader.

Staying ignorant or escaping this pertinent truth of volatility is not going to help. Instead, it is time to start asking yourself the right questions that will enable you to move forward on the journey. Like Thomas Edison said, "There is a way to do it better, find it!"

If you do find yourself in a dead-end situation like shutting down the CX initiative completely or even deferring it indefinitely, reconsider. Here are a few actions you can pursue to stay on the path, maybe at a slower pace but at least making the most of all the effort that has gone in thus far. This will help you stick to your ground of CX.

1. *Never lose touch with your customers*

Staying glued is a good mantra. Whatever the challenge or difficulties may be, customers are not one to be ignored. Let us not forget even customers are part of the same world and going through similar challenges if not the same. Find ways, formal or informal, and create opportunities to establish a genuine connection with them. It doesn't matter what modalities you use but what really would make a difference in customer perception is how you listen to them or share with them. Staying empathetic and personalized attention goes a long way in building trust and healthy relationships.

This might also help you stay realistic about the world of problems that you are battling, and a perspective on how others in the business are tackling similar issues.

2. *Be obsessed with the customer, not your project plan*

Don't get us wrong, we are not recommending to trash your plans. A successful program needs a solid plan. What we are suggesting is, to be open to the idea of making adjustments to it. It will be helpful to accept the change that the situation demands rather than operating from a place of denial or frustration.

Even in the most vulnerable moments when you are feeling a lack of control, stuck, or fearing the unknown, remember all it demands is an adjustment to your plan and not erasing the entire vision. With a firm belief in your CX-Vision, keep moving forward, even if it means taking baby steps. Making small progress is far more important than completely giving up. You always have an option to add rigor when you have a better hold of the situation at a later point.

The bottom line is, stay obsessed with your customers, and don't let your vision go blurry!

3. Stay close to your employees

As explained in earlier chapters, employees are a critical part of the CX ecosystem. It is equally important to keep our workforce engaged as it is to focus on clients. The law of volatility applies to the employees too and a lot of organizations are invested heavily in staying apprised with employee pulse. The term VUCA (volatile, Uncertain, Complex, and Ambiguous) is an important fundamental for future leaders. The recent pandemic has taught everyone a lot of lessons about newer ways of managing work and people.

A disengaged employee is a great risk to business as it would mean low productivity, and bad quality, directly or indirectly impacting customer experience in a negative way. It is required that leaders find time to not only listen to employees, their concerns, and their ideas but also ensure that they feel valued and empowered.

Employee experience is an important part of the Customer Experience framework and an aspect that need focus and attention at all times.

4. Use data for decision making

Difficult situations call for tough decisions. If not handled well, could breed panic, judgments, and distrust, leading to all kinds of chaos and mismanagement. Data is a great savior when it comes to effectively navigating decisions in times of confusion and uncertainty. In the last chapter of Governance, we discussed how important it is to stay objective and drive fact-based decisions.

We must stick to our vision, re-evaluate the goals, and re- assess our metrics and measures. Absolute clarity of key performance indicators and applying them effectively in the process is the bare minimum an organization must adopt to sustain.

5. Communicate Effectively

Effective communication is a bridge between confusion and clarity. Fear and insecurities within the system could be detrimental to seamless operations in business. It makes it easier to maneuver the worst of situations if the communication is kept honest, meaningful, and supported by facts.

Leaders must share the true picture of the impact caused by change and not hesitate to be open about the shift in direction. A genuine and transparent communication helps keep all the unnecessary noise at bay and allows trust to flourish amongst stakeholders.

The three most important competencies for future leaders that are defined today are resilience, empathy, and innovation. Staying grounded and sticking to the basics allows one to thrive in any situation. We hope these guidelines will further assist you in moments of panic and stress and guide you to be resourceful.

To sum it all up, if you still feel lost on your Customer Experience journey, do not know where to begin, or find your efforts not giving desired results, here are a few items you can look at and build on your CX program:

- See if the decision-making discussions are centered around customer's interests
- Look for the right level of leadership responsibility and commitment to the CXM vision
- Start with bringing a cultural shift, keeping customers first, and updating your current policies and governance structure to support it.
- Check if the departments are operating in silos or have a collective aligned view on organization objectives. Organize one on one conversations with functional leaders to know better.
- Start with understanding the customer's point of view on the product or service. Assess the existing voice of customers like feedback, listen

to helpdesk calls, review issue logs or just pick a phone and make a call to the client. Streamline the mechanism of collecting feedback.

- Review customer data to understand customer loyalty metrics. Analyze to find out repeat customers, orders through references, customer lifetime value
- Use and analyze social media to understand, buying behaviors, demographics, or other insights to design your marketing or product strategy.

The most important place to start is to understand the organization's goals and objectives and ensure they are in alignment with Customer Experience outcomes. If you still find yourselves struggling, hire an expert to help you with the CX framework. CXM is the only reliable way to drive customer success and would require some courage and loads of passion to follow.

"In the words of Warren Buffet, "It takes 20 years to build a reputation and five minutes to ruin it. If you think about that, you'll do things differently." – Warren Buffett"

Through this book, we want to encourage you to start having conversations on customer experience management, so don't stop now or ever!

Some Common Terms In Customer Experience, Everyone Should Know

CXM	Customer Experience Management
CX	Customer Experience
EX	Employee Experience
ROI	Return on Investment
Measures	The fundamental unit for classification of raw data like new clients, website visits, etc.
Metrics	Quantifiable measure
Brand Image	Perception of brand formed by the customer
Customer Advocacy	When customers act as champions of brands' product or service and recommends them in their network
Sustainable Business	Able to maintain a desired level of performance
Internal customers	Participate in your business as employees or partners
Omnichannel	Consistent presence across multiple channels
Buyer Persona	Fictional buyer based on identified customer segment
Digital CX	Customer perception of the brand across digital mediums/ technology platforms
Digital Transformation	Using technology to enhance your services or offerings and provide better experiences
Customer segment	Each segment is a category of customers with common characteristics like demographics, behaviors, expectations, preferences, etc
Insights	Inferences drawn from qualitative and quantitative data collected for a better understanding of customer

Voice of Customer	Customer's feedback
TAT	Turn Around Time
CSM	Customer Success Manager
Big Data	Larger, complex datasets from different sources
Machine Learning	Is a subset of artificial intelligence that solves specific tasks by learning from data and making predictions
Artificial Intelligence	Is a machine that is capable of solving problems like a human brain
OTT	Over-the-top – means of providing entertainment content online on the customer's requests and that suits their need or mood.

End Notes

Chapter-1

1. resources for profitability to create a viable and sustainable business from Grønholdt, L., Martensen, A., Jørgensen, S., & Jensen, P. (2015). Customer experience management and business performance. International Journal of Quality and Service Sciences, 7(1), 90–106. doi:10.1108/just-01-2015-0008
2. with them a positive emotion of their experience https://hawkpartners.com/customer-experience/behavioral-economics-is-key-to-customer-experiences/
3. Research across the world demonstrates https://www.superoffice.com/blog/customer-experience- statistics/; https://www.forbes.com/sites/danielnewman/2020/06/23/4-actionable-customer-experience-statistics-for- 2020/?sh=2e67972d1a84; https://www.horizontaldigital.com/insights/customer- experiences-in-emerging-economies
4. 55% of people recommend https://www.superoffice.com/blog/customer-experience- statistics/
5. the law of diffusion of innovation wherein there are different sections of consumers https://www.pinkguava.org/customerexperienceblogs/2019-
6. a Greater understanding of the end-to-end customer interaction process with the business. https://customerthink.com/customer_experience_process/

Chapter-2

1. Different people can have different needs for a product which can be attitudinal, psychological, or behavioral. https://www.qualtrics.com/au/experience-management/research/customer-needs-analysis
2. Harvard professor Clayton Christensen helps in it. It is called "Jobs to be done" https://hbswk.hbs.edu/item/clay-christensens- milkshake-marketing
3. because different cultures have other belief systems, bad behaviors lead to different customer expectations.

https://www.horizontaldigital.com/insights/customer-experience- in-emerging-economies

4. the focus is to protect the fragile and delicate customer trust: Amazon CEO Jeff Bezos Highlights Customer-Centric Retail Strategy (powerreviews.com)

5. expectation matching as per the brand promise https://www.forbes.com/sites/scottdavis/2014/03/27/burberrys-blurred-lines-the-integrated-customer- experience/?sh=74a604fc3cc6

6. tracking, overseeing, and organizing interactions with customers: https://acquire.io/blog/customer-experience-management/

7. Amazon Customer Experience https://www.cmswire.com/customer-experience/3-customer- experience-lessons-brands-can-learn-from-amazon/;https://www.voxco.com/blog/customer-experience-insights-amazon/; https://www.salesforce.com/blog/jeff-bezos-lessons- blog/;

8. 29Billion dollars in profit https://techstory.in/amazon-reports- more-profit-in-2020-compared-to-its-past-three-years-combined- profits/

9. https://thegemba.com/article/building-your-digital-strategy- the-amazon-way

10. four packages were misplaced in 4 million A Forbes contributor Jonathan Salem Baskin has an interesting story to share https://www.forbes.com/sites/jonathansalembaskin/2013/05/09/amazon-earns-customer-loyalty-with-integrity-not-rewards/?sh=352914942148; https://www.nbcnews.com/id/wbna32127300

11. Walt wanted to create an entirely new kind of place https://blog.clientheartbeat.com/disney-customer-experience/

12. Disney Customer Experience https://www.forbes.com/sites/blakemorgan/2020/01/23/5-lessons-from-disneys-magical-customer-experience; https://www.helpscout.com/blog/disney-customer-experience/

Chapter-3

1. On Customer Relationship Management in the organization https://edepot.wur.nl/185571

2. https://timesofindia.indiatimes.com/spotlight/cloudnine-one- of-indias-premium-birthing- centers/articleshow/81269422.cms

3. customer relationship management can provide insights into customer behavior, preferences, and feedback to learn and improve https://blogs.oracle.com/cx/post/how-crm-improves-customer-service-and-the-customer-experience

4. Few recommendations when implementing customer service and CRM solutions https://www.qualtrics.com/experience-management/customer/improve-customer-experience

5. "We aim to "Wow" from https://www.insightssuccess.in/cloudnine-group-of-hospitals- indias-leading-chain-of-maternity-hospitals/

6. VOC and service programs at Cloudnine Hospitals https://www.customerguru.in/customer-centricity-intrinsic- principle-exclusive-interview-mr-rohit-m-co-founder-managing- director-cloudnine/

7. Revenue targets: https://cxotv.techplusmedia.com/trending- news/cloudnine-to-open-10-hospitals-over-next-2-years/

8. "It's our baby" app: https://timesofindia.indiatimes.com/spotlight/cloudnine-one-of- indias-premium-birthing-centers/articleshow/81269422.cms

Chapter-4

1. Talking about how customer success and customer experience differ, https://www.smartkarrot.com/resources/blog/difference- between-customer-success-vs-customer-experience/

2. Amazon is a great example to share and help dig deeper into the concept of customer success. https://www.precisionmarketinggroup.com/blog/customer- success-examples

3. Customer success team in small organizations https://successcoaching.co/blog/building-a-customer-success- team-in-a-startup

Chapter-5

1. Gartner's customer success model https://www.gainsight.com/blog/gartner-2021-market-guide-for- csm-platforms-takeaways/

Chapter-6

1. https://www.xminstitute.com/blog/employees-listen-treat-better/

Reference by Bruce Temkin, XMP, CCXP, is the Head of Qualtrics XM Institute

2. Respect as the key motivator for employees: https://hbr.org/2018/07/do-your-employees-feel-respected
3. Trusting societies and people have more happiness: https://theconversation.com/trusting-societies-are-overall- happier-a-happiness-expert-explains-why-177803
4. Campbell Employee experience https://www.forbes.com/2009/06/23/employee- engagement-conant-leadership-managing-turnaround.html

Chapter-7

1. Forrester research: https://www.ameyo.com/blog/customer-experience-measurement-a-practical-guide-to-measuring-cx
2. The Relationship Between Customer Engagement, Satisfaction, and Loyalty Hani H. Al-Dmour (Princess Sumaya University for Technology, Amman, Jordan), Wasim Khalil Ali (The University of Jordan, Amman, Jordan) and Rand H. Al-Dmour (The University of Jordan, Amman, Jordan) International Journal of Customer Relationship Marketing and Management (IJCRMM) 10(2). DOI: 10.4018/IJCRMM.2019040103
3. Customer perception forms a critical criterion: https://www.clootrack.com/knowledge_base/what-is-customer-perception
4. Research by MIT: How expectation influences perception | MIT News | Massachusetts Institute of Technology
5. Measuring Customer Experience to make an impact: https://www.mckinsey.com/business-functions/operations/our-insights/four-ways-to-shape-customer-experience-measurement- for-impact
6. https://www.ameyo.com/blog/customer-experience- measurement-a-practical-guide-to-measuring-cx
7. Moments of Truth: https://www.mycustomer.com/hr- glossary/moments-of-truth

Chapter-8

1. https://hackernoon.com/metrics-game-framework-5e3dce1be8ac

2. https://uxmag.com/articles/how-to-measure-customer-experience

3. Sustainable Supply Chain through Greater Customer Engagement| Intech Open

4. https://www.interaction-design.org/literature/article/putting- some-emotion-into-your-design-plutchik-s-wheel-of-emotions

5. https://customerthink.com/understanding-the-peak-end-rule- how-it-affects-customer-experience/

6. Standard Metrics: https://www.genroe.com/blog/customer-experience-measurement/15139

7. https://www.forbes.com/sites/blakemorgan/2019/07/29/the-20-best-customer-experience-metrics-for-your-business/?sh=759681b058cc

8. https://www.pointillist.com/blog/how-to-measure-customer-experience-beyond-nps/

9. https://www.gartner.com/smarterwithgartner/how-to-measure-customer-experience/

10. What is the right customer experience for your brand by Luke Williams, Alexander Buoye, Timothy L. Keiningham, and Lerzan Aksoy? Harvard Business Review July,30,2021

11. Kellett (2020), https://exponea.com/blog/customer-lifetime- value-guide/

12. https://www.6seconds.org/2020/08/11/plutchik-wheel-emotions/

13. https://www.mckinsey.com/business-functions/marketing-and- sales/our-insights/prediction-the-future-of-cx

14. case of a manufacturing company https://www.themanufacturer.com/articles/customer-experience- a-new-priority-for-manufacturers

Chapter-9

1. Forrester's predicts report of 2022 https://www.forrester.com/predictions/ for understanding the predictions in detail and knowing your game better.

2. Effective and efficient governance https://clearaction.com/customer-experience-governance-do-this- not-that/

3. https://www.markinblog.com/customer-loyalty-retention- statistics

About The Authors

Dr. Amrinder Kaur

Works as a Consultant, Researcher, and Educator and has worked in diverse academic and corporate profiles for two decades. Along with Consulting in business strategy and customer experience management, she has a research interest in sustainability and entrepreneurship development. She has some worthwhile publications in peer-reviewed journals and keeps collaborating to enhance her efforts in research. She also works as a visiting faculty and Mentor in online and offline management programs for youngsters (Students) and Women for business growth and success. LinkedIn: www.linkedin.com/in/kauramrinder

Ms. Rinku Bhardwaj

With more than two decades of career span, Ms. Rinku Bhardwaj held several leadership roles in Fortune500 companies like Hewitt Associates, Xerox Business Services, etc. Her forte has been processing re-engineering and unlocking hidden potentials in systems and people, maintaining the core philosophy at work of high- performance culture. Along with consulting in business strategy and customer experience, she pursues her passion for coaching by mentoring students and young professionals helping them in making career choices or decisions. She also uses training as a medium to guide self-development. LinkedIn: www.linkedin.com/in/bhardwajrinku